Have Faith...I Will Wait on You

Jeremy Rubin

ISBN: 1492352535
ISBN 13: 9781492352532

Contents

Acknowledgements

To my editors, Les Lemieux and Erinn Rominger, your insights and dedication elevated the final product to a place I couldn't have taken to without you. To Gene Reed, thank you for managing the project. You are a true connector and your contributions are much appreciated. I also want to thank the hundreds of people who took the time to listen to my idea. This was a short story, long before it was a book. Your time, support, and encouragement motivated me to take three and a half years out of my life and complete this journey. Last but not least, I would like to thank God for keeping me and trusting me with such a beautiful story.

Prologue

A Story To Tell

Why did Felicia's son have to come down with the flu on the most important day of my life? Was this some sick, celestial joke? I knew I should have told her earlier! But the timing... The timing was never right. Time. It's a commodity, taken for granted all too often.

I had been bed-ridden for some time now. And I depended on Felicia for everything. I needed her now more than ever.

Bridgett Marie was filling in for her. I hardly knew her, yet her tears broke my heart. She checked up on me more often than necessary. The substitute caretaker was probably overcompensating for the distraction coming from her cell phone.

She switched it to vibrate after the first few calls. Someone was trying to get ahold of her something fierce. Each call inspired the same, uncomfortable routine: the phone vibrated, Bridgette Marie excused herself and, after some very intense whispering and crying, she'd return to ask me what I needed.

I reached for the coffee-stained mug on my small, oak nightstand. The water was stale and lukewarm. But my throat was dry, so I took a sip. Then, I called out, "Bridgette Marie!!!"

Bridgette Marie knocked and slowly opened my squeaky bedroom door.

"Come on in, honey," I said.

Her eyes were red and puffy. She couldn't have been more than twenty years old. She had an even, caramel complexion, high cheekbones, full lips, and jet-black hair pulled back into a neat bun. So beautiful. So vulnerable. She reminded me of the flowers my mother picked from her garden.

With all the professionalism she could muster, she asked, "How can I help you, Mr. O'Dell?"

"Actually, I was wondering how I could help you. If you have an emergency, I'm sure the agency can send someone else."

She interjected frantically, "No, Mr. O'Dell! I'm in a probationary period and if they found out that I... Please don't call the agency, Mr. O'Dell. I need this job."

"OK, we don't need to call anyone. But, can you do me a favor?"

"Anything," she said, gratefully.

"Just call me Joseph."

She replied, "My mother was born and raised in Alabama. She taught me to respect my elders. So, how about I call you Mr. Joseph?"

Her response brought me back to one of the most important moments in my life. It was sobering, to say the least.

Her phone vibrated in her pocket. Half startled, she reached down frantically and silenced it. "I'm so sorry," she softly muttered.

"Bridgette Marie, I will make you a deal. But I need you to turn off your phone first."

Reluctantly, she reached into her pocket, switched off her phone, and placed it on my nightstand.

I said, "Today is your lucky day. We are going to put my declining health on the back burner. For the rest of your shift, you will have just one obligation."

"And what would that be, Mr. Joseph?" she asked.

"Listen to a story," I said, simply.

She quickly interjected, "But, Mr. Joseph, I'm a good worker, I promise. I'm sure there are other things I could do..."

I interrupted, "Trust me. Listening to this story is the most important thing you can do for me."

I asked her to roll a large chest out of my closet. It, like me, was old and worn. The box held my most precious treasures.

She sat on the dingy love seat to the right of my bed. I stared deep into her beautiful, brown eyes and said, "Any, respectable story has a title. And the title of this story is: Have Faith... I Will Wait on You."

I paused and took another sip of the tepid water.

"Have Faith... I Will Wait on You," I said, again. "I repeat it because you remembering the title is of the utmost importance."

"Mr. Joseph, that sounds like the title to a love story," she asserted.

"As a matter of fact, it is the greatest love story no one has ever heard. Well, not until today, that is."

My mind raced back to the beginning, so many years ago. And I tried, unsuccessfully, to hold back the tears that only the past could bring. The salty waters cascaded down the ripples of my weathered cheeks.

"Bridgette Marie, faith is the substance of things hoped for, the evidence of things not yet seen. This is the story of the day I embraced Faith, and met the girl that I would spend the rest of my life with. Chasing after her love would be the toughest thing in the world for me. But, in the end, it was well worth the wait."

Chapter 1
Joseph O'Dell

I hadn't always lived in Tacoma. I grew up in a medium-sized town in Central Washington, located a few hours east of Seattle. Many people passed through our town while travelling between the two cities. It was a great place to take a break from a long road trip. I wouldn't classify our community as one, big rest stop – although it may have been accurate in my grandfather's day.

It was one of those stereotypical, rustic, small towns that exist in so many places across rural America – dusty and common, but unique in its own way. By the time I was in middle school, it had grown; adding to the standard perks that setup to restore a weary, travelling soul. There were a few roadside parks, a great pizza joint and, of course, ice cream from a real, old-fashioned creamery.

For the majority of my youth, I worked in my grandfather's ice cream parlor, O'Dell's Creamery. The creamery was part of the town's character, a piece of living memorabilia that harkened back to a simpler time. My grandfather, the man I was named after, worked hard to establish it.

There was a time when I could have taken pride in carrying on his dream. From an early age, it was simply assumed that I would run the shop one day. But my father, Duke, ruined that notion. His micro-managing, military approach siphoned all the romance and charm out of the creamery for me.

For the most part, Grandpa Joe was nothing more to me than a blurry memory. But my connection to him bloomed nevertheless, and was as authentic as the ice cream he churned by hand. This relationship was solidified when I was about 10 years old, and I came across a large box filled with his artwork.

It was stuffed away, in the stockroom, between some dusty crates and old containers. When I opened the box, I couldn't believe such treasure had been sentenced to life amongst old inventory and miscellaneous junk.

I was impressed by the quality of Grandpa Joe's art, and deeply inspired by the fact that he'd made room in his life for a passion that extended beyond toiling at the creamery. He was a man after my own heart. And his approach was so opposite to Duke's small-minded focus. But, because of Duke's heavy-handed pressure, I thought of the creamery as just a place to work. That is, until *she* graced me with her presence, over 50 years ago.

I remember it like it was yesterday. I swept the red and white-checkered floor with a latent bitterness welling up deep inside of me. Mine was a young man's resentment. It came from forfeiting every, important summer of my remedial life, to keep the family business alive.

I guess that sounds a little dramatic. The business wasn't struggling. As a matter of fact, our red leather booths were always occupied. I can still hear the echoes of bratty kids screaming, "MOM... DAD... CAN WE GO TO O'DELL'S TODAY... PLEASE, PLEASE, PLEASE... CAN WE, CAN WE, CAN WE?"

You know the type: kids that get everything but don't appreciate anything, kids that run around with their ice-cream cones even as their parents beg them to sit down. Those same kids would continue to run. Eventually, their neatly stacked scoops of ice cream would splatter across my red and white-checkered tile floor.

I called the floor "mine" because my father deemed me guardian of its smoothly waxed surface many years before. He'd say, "Joseph O'Dell, this floor is your responsibility. Keep her clean at all times. Cleanliness is next to godliness. And we will be blessed as long as you keep her surfaces spotless." This was just another illusion Duke wanted me to buy into. I was sure God had better things to do.

I started off as an overzealous kid who guarded the floor as though it were an enchanted castle. I was fourteen going on fifteen. I was practically a man. And I had grown numb to Duke's lackluster attempts at making me take more ownership in O'Dell's.

Duke, with his chest puffed out, and his head held high, exclaimed at least three times a day, "Joseph O'Dell, someday this shop will be yours. And you will carry on our family tradition." To hear Duke tell it, it was an epic story, how my grandfather opened the creamery and built it into a virtual cornerstone of our small community. And, of course, being the only child, and a boy, at that, I was the heir to this sugary empire, an empire that was rooted – if not entirely stuck – in the past.

Our creamery was meant to take its customers back to the 50's. And it began with our uniforms. I was forced to wear a white or red short sleeved dress shirt, white Dockers, white apron, white patent leather shoes, and a ridiculous white cafeteria cap that always slumped slightly to the right. That white cap made me feel like a complete dunce. But, in my father's opinion, it was a necessary part of the theme that made the creamery great.

My grandfather's era echoed throughout the entire creamery. When customers entered O'Dell's, their delicate nasal passages were enticed by the smell of freshly prepared waffle cones, and their ears were greeted by the sounds of 1950's "Doo-Wop" groups and barbershop quartets resounding from a big Wurlitzer Jukebox. The walls were solid white with a thick, bold, red stripe dividing them horizontally. These walls, which I had washed on many occasions, were adorned with pictures of Sinatra, Elvis, and other singers and entertainers of my grandfather's heyday. The inside was lined with oversized, red, leather-wrapped booths that could fit four adults on each side. These were a customer favorite. Table rounds were sprinkled about the space between the booths and the front counter. The counter that separated the patrons from the staff was long. Its top was red and bordered by stainless steel. At each end of the counter sat a cash register and a stack of waffle cones. Between these lay a bountiful swath of ice cream heaven.

We offered many delicious foods, refreshments, and treats at O'Dell's. But almost everyone came for the ice cream. We served over 50 flavors of frozen bliss. Our ice cream was still homemade, not ordered in bulk from a distributor like other, newer ice-cream parlors that Duke disdained. In a world of change, my father took great solace in our unwavering approach.

To say that Duke O'Dell was not a huge fan of change was an understatement. Our town had grown considerably since he was a kid. This charming community offered a wide variety of activities outside of the small, downtown area where our creamery was located. The countryside was riddled with wine vineyards and fruit orchards as far as the eye could see. People came from miles around to taste the sweet nectar those hills produced. Our lakes were full of fish and land was cheap. It was a growing oasis, and Duke hated every bit of it. Whenever a new family or business moved into town, he would say, "Joseph, there are only two, good things left in this town: O'Dell's Creamery and the church."

Duke never attended church services. But he contributed money to the church, every month, religiously. His giving was motivated by recognition. When one of the church elders came in for a chilidog or hot fudge sundae, they'd thank my father. Their praise and adoration infused him with an immediate sense of pride. My mother, Gloria, on the other hand, was a lost cause altogether.

Gloria O'Dell, for as long as I can remember, had been what doctors nowadays would diagnose as clinically depressed. Sadly, I possessed very few memories of a happy mother. She was either numb or mad. One day, I built up the courage to ask her why she was always so sad, always locked away by herself in her bedroom. In a soft voice, she simply replied, "I'm fine Joseph. Mind your business."

I knew she wasn't fine, but I left it at that. Duke never tried getting through to my mom. Maybe he knew something I didn't. Maybe he didn't care. I always felt that their marriage was one of obligation. They were a couple emotionally divorced, but kept together by a less tolerant time and place. I assumed that they had been in love at one time. But I hadn't ever seen them show any affection towards each other.

The garden was my mother's escape. Horticulture was an art that her sadness could not impede. She grew gorgeous plants and vegetables that looked like they were auditioning for the cover of *Better Homes and Gardens* magazine. The beauty of my mother's garden was an expression of a love that lay dormant inside of her, a love that I was not afforded the opportunity to feel. Nevertheless, when I strolled through my backyard, I had the opportunity to see my mom for who she really was. Beneath her shell of despair, Gloria was magnificent.

My family's dysfunctions were held to the confines of our home. My father had the entire town convinced (or at least he thought he did) that he and my mom still carried on like newlyweds. When his buddies came into the creamery he would say things like, "The Misses wants to head out to the city next weekend." Or he would boast, "I come home every night to a six-course meal. I tell the little lady time and time again that it isn't necessary, but she loves to spoil me." Hearing these blatant lies made me sick to my stomach. Who was he trying to impress? The same people whispered about how my mom hadn't left her house in years. They played along for Duke's sake. But, in the end, he made himself look foolish.

I guess I shouldn't judge my parents too harshly. My daily routine was a lie, as well. Every day I worked at the creamery, I was mislead-ing Duke. I did not by any means want to take over the shop. I didn't even like being there. Papa Pete's ice-cream feed was the only place I found peace.

Papa Pete was the youth pastor at First Hope Church. He didn't like to be called a "pastor". He felt the title was too formal. Every Wednesday night, he'd invite out kids from our junior high to eat free ice cream. After he filled their tummies, he fed their souls with encouragement.

Sarah Dwyer never missed one of Papa Pete's ice-cream feeds. Sarah was Pastor Paul's daughter. Pastor Paul worked alongside Papa Pete. She was my second best friend and the funniest girl I had ever met. Sarah was a tomboy, but there was beauty underneath her boyish attitude and clothes. She had jet-black hair that was constantly pulled back into a ponytail, pale porcelain skin, and the clearest blue eyes I had ever seen. I didn't know it then, but she would become a major part of my life.

On Sundays, I usually rode my bike down to one of the lakes located just outside of town, in order to indulge my second love: poetry. I tried to avoid the more popular lakes. They were full of people boating, inner tubing, and enjoying a whole host of other activities to which I was never invited. My favorite was Lonely Lake. I'm sure its official name wasn't "Lonely". I gave it the name because I never saw anyone else there. It was my own, little secret.

I hid my poetry from my father. Duke didn't think it was an appropriate pastime for a young man. I'm sure he thought I was skipping rocks and jumping off docks. I wasn't. I was searching for inspiration in the still waters. Maybe one day the words that I labored over might matter to someone else. Maybe, just maybe...

The few people I shared my writing with said I was gifted. I wrote about things big and small. Sometimes the poems were about abstract ideas, and other times they were about things tangible and real. No matter what the topic, the shoreline of the lake provided the perfect backdrop for artistry. I escaped through my writing. But no matter how far away it took me I still had to go back to the shop on Monday.

Today was one of those Mondays. Bitterly, I swept the floor until I was greeted by the sound of the shop bell. I ushered the last of the dust bunnies into the dustpan. I expected to seat another patron at one of our booths. But this was not a paying customer. Nope, it was my best friend, Little PJ. He was there to collect his free, daily ice-cream cone, complements of me.

Little PJ was born Jessie Montague Preston. This was quite a mouthful for anyone. And, as we already had both a "Jessie" and a "JP" in our town, Jessie Montague Preston received "Little PJ" as his moniker, due to his lack of seniority and stature. Little PJ was awkwardly small, with red hair and more than his fair share of freckles. Our friendship, at first, spawned from obligation.

My junior high had a funny tradition. At the beginning of each year, our school would hold a raffle to see who would share lockers. Our 7th grade year, Little PJ and I both scored bullies for locker partners. By the end of the day, I had a black eye and Little PJ had spent two class periods trapped in his locker. Principle Gordon, figuring we had a lot in common after the bullying occurred, decided to make us locker mates. And from that, inauspicious beginning, a real friendship grew.

Little PJ came from a very poor family. He was the youngest of six kids. His eldest siblings were already married with kids of their own. Little PJ would be the first to tell you that he was an accident.

The Preston house was crowded. Eleven people lived in a singlewide at Rosy Glenn Trailer Park. There was nothing rosy about that place, at all. His parents and older brothers worked for one of Stones' apple orchards just outside of town. Little PJ never really got an appropriate level of attention, but he never used this as an excuse. By the 9th grade, he had more education than everyone else in his house, combined.

Needless to say, Little PJ could not afford ice cream. So, if anyone deserved a frozen treat, it was him. But Duke did not let me give away ice cream, even to someone as deserving as Little PJ. Any time that I took care of anyone in this manner, the cost had to come out of my own pocket. It was a small price to pay for a lifelong buddy if you ask me.

Business was slow, so I asked to take a break and hang with Little PJ while he ate. Duke barked, "That's fine. But keep it to ten minutes." Before he left to balance the inventory, he said, "Joseph, you know the routine. Your break is over when *paying* customers come through the doors."

After my father left, I asked, "So, what do you want?" Little PJ pressed his small hands against the glass and hunted through the flavors. He knew that putting his hands on the glass was against the rules, but he couldn't help himself (plus my father wasn't around to remind him). This moment was the height of his day, so I never spoiled it for him.

He took two, long minutes hemming and hawing over the sweet selection. Finally, he hesitantly said, "Cookies and cream."

I held the scoop of ice cream parallel to the counter. Then, in a mockingly serious tone, I asked him, "Would you like this in one of our freshly prepared waffle cones or a cup sir? You look like a cup sort of guy. Am I right?"

"C'mon Joseph," he said. "Don't joke about my waffle cones." I handed him the cone, rang up the sale, and took the total owed out of my tip jar.

The shop bell rang just before I could join Little PJ. I thought to myself, "Why me? All I want to do is hang out with my buddy." I looked up to see which local, traveler, or random vagabond I had to help when *she* entered.

The girl of my dreams had just walked through the doors of my grandfather's creamery. She was followed by a lady who appeared to be her mother. The sight of the girl almost caused Little PJ to drop his ice-cream cone, while I was struggling to pick my jaw off of the floor.

I don't mean to obsess over the way she looked, but God didn't make girls like her in our town. I couldn't put my finger on her ethnicity. She was the best of everything, wrapped up in an angel's shell.

The bright, yellow sundress she wore was dim compared to her radiance. She had blondish-brown hair that sat just below her elegant shoulders, hazel-green eyes, and an olive complexion. She even had six dimples that scattered about her face when she smiled. Her mannerisms revealed her age to be close to mine, but she was physically developed beyond her years. She stood about 5'8" tall (I knew this because I was 5'6" and she had at least two inches on me). She was stunning.

Barely able to breathe, I asked her mother, "How can I help you?" Her mom was a weathered reflection of her. I didn't dare address the girl. I would've just stumbled over my words and embarrassed myself. Little PJ watched in delight as I bumbled through the experience.

Her mom gave a bold introduction. "Hi. My name is Kathy. But you can call me Kat. And this is my daughter, Meadow. And your name is?"

"My name is Joseph, Ma'am," I said, timidly.

"Do I look like a Ma'am to you?" she asked, offended.

"No Ma'am... Oops. I mean, no Mrs. Kathy."

She gave me a once-over and replied, "I prefer Kat over Kathy, but I guess you can call me Mrs. Kat, if you like."

I timidly responded, "OK, Mrs. Kat."

Mrs. Kat had a classic case of "forever young syndrome". I had seen this ailment many times before – moms that came into the creamery with their daughters, in hopes that someone would ask whether they were sisters. They run the day's errands with their daughters, just to catch the tail end of the attention.

Mrs. Kat fit this description to a tee. Her short skirt flaunted her varicose vein-covered legs. Her bright green tank top exposed more cleavage than I was comfortable with. Her wrists and neck were heavily dressed with costume jewelry, and her face was covered in heavy, dark makeup. Her hair was dyed brown with obvious blonde highlights. But its grey roots exposed that she hadn't visited the hairdresser in quite some time.

Mrs. Kat looked at the menu while Meadow stood by her side, smiling. After a couple of uncomfortable, silence-filled moments, Mrs. Kat said, "Joseph, I know what my daughter wants. Her favorite ice cream is pralines 'n' cream. But I don't know what I want. What should I get?"

I replied with my father's, patented copout, "All of our ice cream is good."

Then she pointed in Little PJ's direction (he was startled by her assertiveness) and said, "I'll have what he's having!"

Curious, I asked, "Don't you want to know what he's having first?"

"Nope. You said all the ice cream is good. I want a scoop of what he's having in a waffle cone and a cup of pralines 'n' cream. My beautiful daughter doesn't like waffle cones. She is beautiful isn't she?" I could feel my ears and face start to turn red.

Meadow nudged her mom and said, "Do you have to embarrass me everywhere we go?"

"You know you're beautiful. And Joseph knows you're beautiful, too. Why do you think he's blushing? The apple doesn't fall far from the tree, does it, Joseph?" My forehead began to sweat and my throat dried up. I rescued myself by following protocol.

"Is that going to be for here or to go?" I asked, after scooping up their order.

Mrs. Kat replied, "Joseph, we are in a hurry. So, make it to go?" She looked at Meadow and said, "Let's get out of here, honey. These local boys can't keep their eyes off of us."

As they walked out of the shop, Meadow turned around and mouthed out, "Sorry," so that her mom couldn't hear her. Then, she said, "Thank you."

Little PJ laughed. "Joseph, how do you do it? You're great with the girls," he said, sarcastically.

"Don't make me kick you out of my shop," I retorted.

Little PJ sensed that I was more serious than usual, so he left me alone.

I sat at the booth as he finished his ice cream. He carried on a conversation with me, but I couldn't tell you what he said if my life depended on it. I was too upset with myself to pay attention. There were so many questions I should have asked her. At the bare minimum, I should have asked if she was new to town. Be that as it may, I still felt like I was in a dream. All I could hope for was that I would run into Meadow again.

"Have you ever experienced love at first sight, Bridgett Marie?"

"I don't believe in that stuff anymore," she said, in a frustrated tone.

"You are far too young to speak like that, young lady. You are a beautiful and talented girl..."

"How do you know?" she interrupted. "You just met me!" Realizing the tone she took with me, she said, "I'm sorry, Mr. Joseph. I didn't mean to come off so disrespectfully."

"That's quite alright," I said, with a smile. "You're right. I don't know you. But, you remind me of someone I cared for very much. And, if you're anything like her, you don't give yourself enough credit."

Bridgett Marie bowed her head. I placed my finger underneath her chin and raised her pretty face. A single tear rolled down her cheek and into the nook of her mouth.

"And, if I'm right," I continued, "you will do something special. In time, everyone will see how bright you are."

She grabbed my hand and said, "Thank you Mr. Joseph."

I nestled my back deeper into the pillows. My body grew uncomfortable, but I couldn't let that stop me. There was too much at stake. I cleared my throat, "Uh um... Where was I?"

Chapter 2

Summer's End

I woke up to the obnoxious cry of my alarm clock. It was Sunday, a day I did not have to struggle to get up. This was my day off. Despite all the great things I had planned, I couldn't help feeling down.

I never grew accustomed to waking up in my bedroom. It was the basement of our house. And it was a fairly large space for one person to abide in. My living in that basement spawned from an epic disagreement between my parents.

At one time, Duke had great expectations for this room. His friends bragged, "Your old man turned that basement into the place to be!" It was a man's oasis and a lot cheaper than patronizing the local pub. Duke went through a great deal of trouble to remodel the basement.

My father was an avid UW (University of Washington) football fan in a town of WSU (Washington State University) supporters. He loved every minute of it. The UW was where my father intended to go; that was until his injury. He was an All-American running back in high school. When his senior year rolled around, WSU made no attempt to recruit him.

The UW recruited my father heavily. They were the first school to offer him a scholarship. But Duke blew out his knee halfway through his senior season of high school.

UW was very gracious. Confident his body would heal; they offered him academic and leadership scholarships. Despite the encouragement of the coaching staff and my grandfather, Duke never went to college. He settled to work at the shop.

Duke's renovations to the basement began with the walls. He painted the unfinished sheetrock bright white. Then, he lined its perimeter with perfectly level, purple and gold striping. Duke put a UW Husky helmet decal on the main wall, opposite the stairs. It was larger than life, and grabbed the attention of visitors that trampled down the beaten stairs. He covered the cold concrete floor with beige shag-carpet. It was long enough to get caught in-between unsuspecting toes. The room's theme was a poke at all my father's WSU buddies.

Living in the basement bordered on eerie. It doubled as a room for Duke's forgotten "stuff". On the right side of the room was a book-shelf filled with dusty literature. To the right of the bookshelf was my father's old trophy case.

Occasionally I looked at Duke's old pictures and trophies in awe. How could we share the same DNA? Duke was such a stud in his day. Come to think of it, he never lost his football build. He stood 6'3" and weighed around 240 pounds – although he liked to remind me that a solid 195 pounds was his playing weight. He may have lost a step or two, but Duke still had his barrel chest and massive forearms.

My father had a commanding presence. When he walked into a room people paid attention. I often heard customers refer to Duke as handsome. He had blue eyes, a full head of jet-black hair that was just starting to gray around his temples, and a strong jaw line. I, on the other hand, took after my mother.

I was 87 pounds soaking wet with two Christmas hams strapped to my back. I did not get Duke's baby blues. My eyes were a plain brown and easily overlooked. I was *just* average. The evidence was overwhelming.

"Mr. Joseph, it seems like you were pretty down on yourself," Bridgett Marie said.

"You're right. I was. Like anything, self-worth takes time to build. I was like a lot of young people. I was reactive – a product of my environment. My happiness was measured by a lot of things that didn't matter."

Bridgett Marie pondered my words for a moment, and then asked, "What changed?"

"With age comes wisdom, gained from experiences. True happiness comes when you're at peace with yourself, first."

She asserted, "It just doesn't seem realistic, especially with all the stuff that gets thrown at us..."

I interrupted, "Bridgett Marie, finding peace isn't easy. It comes once you're honest with yourself. It comes when you can look in the mirror and be comfortable with the person staring back at you."

Sadly, she asked, "What if you've done something you aren't proud of?"

I smiled and said, "We've all done things we aren't proud of. Acceptance and perfection are two very different things."

"That makes sense, Mr. Joseph."

On the left side of the room lay an old popcorn maker and my grand-father's antique writing desk. The desk was a relic, and the basement's oldest tenant. It was passed down from my grandfather to Duke. And being that Duke had no interest in the desk and no intention of passing away any time soon, I inherited it prematurely. Gaining it by default did not cheapen my pride in owning the desk. It was the most precious of all my room's appointments.

The writing desk was carved from solid oak and had a medium com-plexion. Its top slanted 15 degree's upward from start to finish. It wore its weary age gracefully. The desk had four large drawers on the right side of it. Each drawer had metal handles that had worn through their bronze finish. These handles were useless now. Nature had long-since warped the wood causing the drawers to swell shut. However, it had a small fifth drawer that was located just below the desktop. It still had a bit of play on its tracks.

I would have liked to use this drawer to store my pencils, paper clips, and maybe a poem or two. It didn't seem to have suffered the same fate as its wooden counterparts. I asked Duke if he had a key for the drawer on a number of occasions. He always got irritated and, in a gruff voice, responded, "I don't have a key for the damn drawer!" I guess it didn't matter. Having the opportunity to write on the same desk that my grandfather had practiced his art upon was good enough for me.

The pictures he created were a manifestation of his love and guiding wisdom in my life. Maybe I'm biased, but even 'till this day, I have never seen anyone execute a style of art as inspiring and thought provoking as my grandfather's. He left behind many, extraordinary works.

One piece had a young man standing at the edge of a cliff, alone. His clothes were ripped and torn, his white shirt was dingy, and he had no shoes or socks. The haunting light of the moon gave warning to how close he was to death. The cliff's edge gave way to a 200-foot drop-off and, at its end, laid an angry sea crashing against sharp rocks. The young man stood on his tippy-toes reaching for an unseen treasure. At the bottom of the canvas the words "Reach for the Stars" were written in silver.

When I wrote on the very desk my grandfather labored over, I imagined him sitting there beside me. What great conversations we would have had, artist to artist, grandfather to grandson. Why couldn't Duke embrace me like the idea of my dead grandfather?

I got dressed to the sounds of Duke's snoring. The vent that led to the basement was somehow connected to his room. Every night it was a race to get to bed first. Duke had a snore that sounded like a hog's mating call. There was nothing pretty about it.

I grabbed my socks and sat on the large, green and blue flannel couch that occupied the middle of the room. The couch separated my bed from the pool table, and was Little PJ's favorite attraction.

Little PJ spent the night at my house at least three times a week. It was a win-win situation. For Little PJ, my room was the Ritz in comparison to the accommodations in his home. And, for me, well, I appreciated the company.

A certain sense of freedom came over Little PJ every time he visited. It was as if a weight was lifted off his shoulders. Here, he didn't feel out of place. On the contrary, Little PJ felt right at home. When the old, flannel couch folded out, it revealed a king-sized bed, and Little PJ devoured the large space with his tiny body. Every morning when we woke up, I could see him sprawled across the bed as if he was trying to make sure that no square inch of the mattress went to waste. It was humbling to see that something as insignificant as an old hide-a-bed could give someone such satisfaction.

I headed upstairs to the kitchen. The light shined through the window over the sink and revealed an empty kitchen table. The table was a waste of space. Our family never ate together, even on Thanksgiving. I grabbed a couple of bananas and headed for the door.

I heard the footsteps of my mother as I grabbed the handle. Her dead, brown eyes overlooked me. She headed toward the sliding doors at the back of the living room. She wore a straw hat and gloves. As usual, Gloria O'Dell was preparing for a long day in the garden. The season was coming to an end and it was the only thing that kept her happy.

"Bye mom," I hastily threw back. I didn't want to distract her from the one thing keeping her content. She didn't give me a "goodbye" in return. I was used to it.

I grabbed my bike off the side of the house and pedaled for the lake. It was a day where fall mingled with summer to make for a fresh and mild climate. As always, I was excited for a day at the lake. I ate my bananas, while steering with my opposite hand.

Deep in thought, I rode the trails of the untamed countryside. I had Papa Pete's words on my brain. He posed a question at the last ice-cream feed.

"Will you be who you are intended to be?" he'd asked the attendees, confidently.

Most of the students had looked at each other in a sort of dazed confusion. He asked the question repeatedly, for effect. Then, he explained, "Everyone is born to do something great. The key to fulfilling your purpose is in the three 'F' words."

I laughed to myself, remembering the shock on everyone's faces.

He continued, "Not that 'F' word."

The entire creamery broke into laughter. Papa Pete said, "The three 'F' words are fear, faith, and forged. Fear is a natural response. A life without fear is not a life worth living. Faith is believing in yourself when everything and everyone else does not. Our faith helps us overcome our fear. And Forged is becoming a person worthy of greatness. It is tough, even painful at times. But it is a requirement for those who want to be who they are intended to be. Many are called but few are chosen."

Passion and creativity laced his every word. Despite his familiar demeanor, he was somewhat of an enigma to me. I don't know what brought him to our small community. He was a black man in a white town. It wasn't a big deal, but some days you couldn't help but notice – at least until he interacted with you.

Somehow, Papa Pete didn't see color. He operated in a world where only love existed. When you got within earshot of him you had no choice but to operate in love too. He was a handsome and charismatic guy with a solid build. He had dark brown hair that he kept short and neat, hazel eyes, and a contagious smile.

"His smile was a lot like yours, Bridgett Marie."

"Thank you, Mr. Joseph."

Little PJ was fishing when I arrived. And Sarah joined us after church. We wanted to get one, last, free day in before school started. I sat a couple of yards from Little PJ. I didn't want to get hooked as he casted. I whipped my notebook from my backpack. Sarah joined Little PJ on his fishing expedition. So I had some quiet time to myself.

I had Meadow on my mind. So I wrote something entitled, *Just Passing Through.*

———❦———

"Thank you, Bridgett Marie, for rolling my old, treasure chest out of my closet," I said, nodding at the battered trunk.

"No problem, Mr. Joseph," she replied, though she'd labored a bit over the box as it was heavy and awkward to move. Bridgett Marie had rolled the chest to the side of the bed she was sitting on. I asked her to open it. I tried to lean over, but my tired muscles couldn't handle it.

"I've got it," she said, helpfully.

"There is a notebook with a red cover..."

"Found it!" she said, excited. She gasped, "Is that the same notebook?"

"Yes," I answered, with a smile.

I flipped a few pages and handed her the notebook. "Please read it," I said. "My eyes aren't what they used to be."

Bridgett Marie stared down at the hand-scrawled passage and read:

> My routine was interrupted today
> On account of the oddest thing
> Her allure took my breath away
> Then, her smile resuscitated me
>
> Hazel-green eyes and blondish-brown hair
> Make boys do foolish things
> Like stumble over their words, gawk, and stare
> The awkwardness that young love brings
>
> You disturbed this ordinary town
> And left without any conciliation
> Now, olive complexions and yellow sundresses
> Lie stitched in this boy's imagination

Sadly, it was all just a ploy
Some things are too good to be true
Don't get your hopes up, country boy
Beauty like that is just passing through

"It's beautiful. How old were you when you wrote this?" she asked.

"Fourteen."

"Fourteen year old boys don't write like this," she said with a smile.

"I can't explain it. The words just came to me. They always did. If you ask me, they weren't my thoughts, but rather, the whispers of angels. All I had to do was write down their messages."

"You have a gift, Mr. Joseph."

"Everyone has a gift. What's yours?" I asked, intrigued.

"I don't have anything that comes close to yours," she said, assertively. "My mother always said that my biggest talent was getting people to open up to me. I'm... Or, at least I was a social butterfly. I'm not sure if I would call that a gift..."

"I think it is," I interrupted. "The world has lost the human touch. We can do or buy most anything without talking to a single person. You, Bridgett Marie, can connect with people, a lost art, and make them feel comfortable in their own skin. That seems like a special gift, to me."

Chapter 3

Back to School

It took everything in my body to get up Monday morning. The alarm clock offended my ears with its annoying shrill. I extended my left hand from beneath the covers and beat it until it stopped squawking. The clock was a necessary evil. I needed to get up for the first day of school. Groggy, I rose from my slumber. I woke up Little PJ on my way to the bathroom. He had decided to sleep over. I was exhausted. We had stayed up most of the night, talking.

We got dressed, ate some cold cereal, and biked off to Gene Reeves Junior High. "Do you think we'll share lockers this year?" Little PJ asked as we rode.

"Sure hope so," I answered.

Excited, Little PJ said, "Can you believe we'll be in high school soon?"

"I'm in no hurry to get to high school," I admitted, advising, "Let's just try to survive *this* year, first."

We arrived at the modest, junior high campus, and all the usual faces were present and accounted for. While all our classmates gossiped about who had a crush on whom and which teachers were the meanest, Little PJ and I had very important business to attend to.

The science teacher, Mr. Flak, was at the entrance of the building with a box in his hand. Mr. Flak was ex-military. He had a shiny, bald head, a grey mustache, and blue eyes. He walked taller than most, and was a firm and fair man.

"Go ahead boys, pull your locker number," he said.

I protested, "But Mr. Flak, Little PJ and me really want to be locker partners again. Do you think we can work something out?"

Mr. Flak shook his head and said, "Look, the two of you are going to follow the rules just like everyone else. I know you guys were bullied a couple years back, but don't worry. You're at the top of the food-chain now."

We were frustrated, but could see that he wasn't going to budge. Reluctantly, we took our turns collecting slips of paper to see which lockers would be ours for the year. I unfolded my slip.

"I have locker number three," I said. "What about you?"

"Sorry, Joseph. I pulled number eleven."

I felt disappointed as we headed down the hall in separate directions. The first bell rang just as I put my supplies away. I was bumped a thousand times, by over-zealous kids, rushing to claim the best spots in their lockers. They didn't have the foresight of Little PJ and me. Rookies!

One guy bumped me so hard I spun 180 degrees. What I saw next floored me. It couldn't be... it was! Meadow was walking down the halls of my school. I was so nervous I couldn't speak. I observed her as she scanned the top of the lockers. Meadow walked until she almost bumped into me. Looking up, she playfully slapped me on the shoulder.

"Hey... I remember you. You are the guy from the ice-cream shop. No... No... Don't tell me. You're Joseph, right? I'm Meadow in case you don't remember," she said, with a smile.

"I remember you. You came in the shop with your mom," I answered, nervously.

After checking my locker number, she said, "It looks like it's me and you."

Frantically, I pulled my stuff out to make room for hers. I remember making a mess all over the floor. "Joseph, you don't have to do that," she protested. "I can find a place for my things."

"No it's ok."

I decided this would be a good time to politely dismiss myself. "Well, I guess I'll be heading to class," I muttered.

"Do you have Mrs. Pittman's class, by chance?" she asked, hopefully.

"Yeah, I do."

"I do too. You're stuck with me," she said, playfully. I nodded my head in disbelief.

I was in utter shock. With all the excitement, I didn't see Sarah and Little PJ sitting a couple of rows behind us. They pointed and giggled at my expense. Little PJ was probably telling her that I had a crush on Meadow. The last bell rang as the class shuffled in.

Our classroom was basic. Time had tinted the mostly bare walls yellow. A large desk sat at the front of the room and behind the desk a large blackboard sat mounted on the wall. The room was pretty plain, but there was nothing plain about Mrs. Pittman.

Mrs. Pittman stood 4 foot 10 inches, but her large heart made up for her small stature. She wore glasses with thick, brown frames, and sported short, black hair. She was a teacher who truly cared about her students.

"Good morning class," she said.

"Good morning, Mrs. Pittman," the class responded, in unison.

She took roll call. Then she said, "I would like to introduce a new student to you, class. She's new to town, so let's make her feel welcome. Meadow, please come up and tell us a little bit about you."

The boys were practically drooling over her as she strolled to the front. She spoke with a confidence that bordered on bravado. "Hi. I'm Meadow, and me and my mom moved here a couple of weeks ago. We live in a house by Rosy Glenn."

Oh my goodness. I knew exactly where she lived. It was the old Thompson house. It was the only house by Rosy Glenn Trailer Park. I rode past it hundreds of times on my way to Little PJ's. That house wasn't fit to live in. Maybe her mom paid someone to fix it up, I thought, hopefully.

"I'm from Seattle, so this place is a little different," she continued. "Let's see... hmm. I grew up learning ballet and ice-skating, but I've never skated on a frozen lake. I heard that it gets cold enough to do that here. So I'd like to try it. And... I guess that's it."

Everyone clapped politely.

"Does anyone have any questions for Meadow?" Mrs. Pittman asked.

Elijah John raised his hand first. He asked, "Have you had time to do anything around town yet?"

"I haven't had time to do much. I went to Joseph's creamery though," she pointed at me and smiled.

My popularity was growing by the minute. I had just been endorsed by the hot, new girl. This was great! Sally watched Meadow with jealousy written all over her face. Without raising her hand, she cut in. "What do your mom and dad do?"

Meadow answered, "My mom is looking for work. She hurt her back in an accident a little while ago, so there are a lot of things she can't do."

She paused briefly and looked off to the left. She stared into space for a moment, and then went on, a little more softly, "My dad was... is a banker. But he decided that he didn't want a family anymore, and he gave us just enough money..." suddenly realizing that her comments revealed too much, Meadow said, "I'm sorry, Mrs. Pittman."

An uncomfortable silence came over the class as Meadow made her way back to her seat. Mrs. Pittman interjected, "Give Meadow a hand again, class." Our clapping broke the tension and brought the atmosphere back to normal.

"It's time for your first assignment. Take out a pen and paper to jot down some notes," Mrs. Pittman instructed.

We shuffled through our supplies as Mrs. Pittman dictated. "Your assignment is to write a report about your locker partner. Most of you know each other on the surface, but I want you to go deeper. What makes your locker partner special? It doesn't need to be long, just a few paragraphs. Each of you will take turns presenting this Friday."

Meadow leaned toward me and whispered, "I guess there's no getting rid of me."

I smiled and turned away. I didn't want her to notice me blushing. I thought to myself, "How could this get any better?"

The rest of the day flew by like a blur. Meadow and I were joined at the hip. She ate lunch with Little PJ, Sarah, and I. And we hung out every recess. I asked myself, over and over, "Why is she hanging out with me?" I assumed it was because I was familiar, and I knew the lay of the land.

After school, we filed out of the doors of Gene Reeves. Pastor Paul was waiting for Sarah. He dropped her off and picked her up every day, even though they only lived a stone's throw away. Then it was down to Little PJ, Meadow, and Me. I usually rode my bike with Little PJ to O'Dell's. But this was no ordinary day.

Meadow touched my shoulder and asked, "Can you guys walk me home? Or, at least to O'Dells? I think the shop is on the way."

"Yes!" I blurted out, immediately. "I mean, no. I mean, at least until the shop," I said, scattered.

There I went, tripping over my words again. Meadow giggled. There was no hiding the fact that she made me nervous. I signaled with my head to Little PJ to move on without us.

Picking up on it, he improvised. "Hey Joseph... I just remembered I need to get going. My mom needs help with a few things."

"OK, Little PJ."

We thought we were so smooth. But we weren't. I worked my way over to the bike rack and grabbed my bike. "Meadow, where's your bike?" I asked.

"I don't have one," she said, softly.

Walking from school to Rosy Park wasn't some easy endeavor. By bike, it was a 10 to 12-minute commute. And it was a grueling, 40-minute trek, on foot. I couldn't believe she'd walked so far that morning.

"Why don't you ride mine," I offered.

"I can't do that," she declined. "It's your bike..."

"Ok then, we'll both walk," I said.

"Whatever you say, Joseph," she chuckled.

Casual conversation with a real girl was foreign to me. I talked to Sarah all the time, but she didn't count. We had known each other for years. The only 'new girls' I spoke to were travelers visiting the shop. Even then, the conversation was limited to, "Would you like hot fudge or caramel on your sundae?"

Meadow was harder to talk to. She was comfortable in her own skin. Her words came out with ease and confidence. I was captivated.

I didn't engage in friendly conversation without taking the necessary precautions. I could be clumsy. So I placed my bike between us. I didn't want to step on her foot or bump into her.

We arrived at the shop in no time. I didn't want that moment to end. Meadow said with a smile, "Thanks for walking with me, Joseph. Don't' spill a milkshake on someone, and totally embarrass yourself."

A light bulb went off as she walked away. "Meadow!" I called out. "Yes?"

"Take my bike," I suggested.

"Don't be silly. You hardly know me," she said.

"You can meet me with it in the morning," I said, ignoring her objections. At her uncertain look, I added, "Please."

She fidgeted for a moment, and said, "I like you, Joseph."

She gave me a playful smile, but I could see true gratitude just below the surface.

"Just take the bike, please," I said, before waving goodbye.

"Ok, Joseph. I'll see you tomorrow. You better not be late," she joked.

Suddenly, I was slapped with reality. I was running late. I scurried to the back and changed into my uniform. I carried myself with a new confidence. I hadn't felt that good in... well... I hadn't ever felt that good. Duke stood at the counter. He never admitted it, but my shift was a necessary break for his weary feet. As usual, Duke had me man the counter while he balanced the books in the back room. If you ask me, this was his designated naptime.

Duke called out, "Hey, I'm going to need you to stay late tonight. I told Coach Jimmie to send Logan Stone and his buddies down to eat, on us. They should take state this year!"

I thought to myself, "Big whoop... who cares if they take state". What a downer. The greatest day of my life was about to come crashing down. Logan and his thugs would put me through hell soon. They harassed me every time they came to the shop. And Duke let them. Maybe he thought it was good for me, or maybe it was a "jock thing". Either way, I couldn't stand Logan or anyone he associated with. He had everything, and I mean EVERYTHING, but he didn't appreciate anything.

Logan was a god in our town. He stood 6 feet 3 inches tall and had the body of a superhero. He had sandy-blonde hair, blue eyes, and, on top of being a star quarterback, Logan was rich. His father grew up in our town, but made it big in real estate. He owned land in Washington and California. Most of the local orchards were his, as well. Mr. Stone always planned to keep Logan in our small town. He felt the environment would keep the boy grounded. Logan was projected to lead Windham High to the state championships, as a junior.

He had everything, but he was cruel and shallow. Still, somehow, he had become the apple of my father's eye.

Duke coached during football season. He walked on their field a hero. My father still held many of the records at Windham. He had carried the team to the state championship more than anyone else. The players took to him, especially Logan. He was the son Duke always wanted to have.

It was 15 minutes 'till closing when I heard the "Ring-Ring" of the shop bell. Little PJ finally decided to show up. "Where have you been?" I asked, in place of a regular welcome.

"I had stuff to do. Plus, I was giving you and your girlfriend some alone time," he teased.

"She isn't my girlfriend," I responded.

"You could sure say that again," he said, meanly.

Hurt, I coldly responded, "Just pick out what you want."

"Joseph, you never know. You *might* have a chance," Little PJ laughed. Realizing I was in no mood to joke, he foolishly decided to press his luck. "After all," he snickered, "Everyone loves the ice-cream man." He howled with laughter.

"That's it," I snapped. "Get out."

"Joseph! Quick... quick... I'm not going to make it." Little PJ dropped to the ground, faced down.

"Get up, clown."

"No... not until you say sorry," he wheezed.

Puzzled, I asked, "Say sorry for what?"

"Say sorry for wearing that ugly hat."

"I'm sorry." In spite of myself, I could not help but giggle. Little PJ always knew how to make me laugh.

Suddenly, our laughter was interrupted by a 400 horsepower V8.

They were here.

Little PJ rose from the floor and darted to the booth furthest from the door. I didn't blame him. He didn't want to get caught in the crossfire.

Duke made his way from the back room. He'd heard the engine too. His face beamed with pride as they approached the doors. Mine prepared for impact.

Logan Stone, Big Mike, and Eric Boose entered O'Dell's like they owned the place. Eric was an All-State defensive lineman and the anchor of the defense. He was extremely quiet, and the nicest of the bunch. Big Mike was vile. His attitude stunk almost as bad as his armpits. No one had the courage to stand up to him. His 340 pounds stretched across a 6 foot 5 inch frame.

Excited, Duke shook Logan's hand and said, "You ready to win state, son?"

"You know it, Coach O. Thanks for letting us come and eat."

"Anything for you, boys," Duke said, confidently.

My father stretched his pointer finger in my direction and barked, "You see that guy? He is here to serve you. And like I told Coach Jimmie, whatever you want is on the house."

"Thanks, Coach O," they said, in unison.

My father retreated to the back and threw me to the wolves. The entire arrangement made me sick. Duke wasn't a real coach and they were just pretending to be nice. They were jerks. It didn't take long before the abuse began.

They rumbled over to a booth while Logan heckled, "Hey, water boy... oops, I mean, water girl. Get over here!"

I took a positive approach. I walked over with a beat in my step. Maybe that would change how they treated me. I manufactured a smile and said, "Welcome back, guys. What can I get started for you?"

Big Mike sat on the outside of the booth. He stood up, blocking my view of everyone else. He'd been at practice for hours, and I could smell the sweat that had permeated his ripe body. He poked his finger into my chest and asked, "What's the special, water girl?"

I made the mistake of standing up for myself. "Don't call me that," I said, assertively.

Little PJ peered over the booth he was cowering in. He tried his best to watch without being noticed. In one, quick motion, Big Mike slapped my hat off with his bear claw. I felt the force as his swing cut through the air over my head.

He sneered, "If I call you a water girl, then that's your name, water girl. Besides, I just did you a favor. That hat was as ugly as your face! You should be worshiping me right now," they bellowed, together.

I could feel tears welling up in my eyes. I knew if I cried, it would just get worse. I kept my mouth shut and retreated to the counter. 10 chilidogs, 8 orders of chili cheese fries, 6 ice-cream sundaes, and 1000 insults went by before they'd had their fill. To top it off, they left a gigantic mess. I thought to myself, "Where was Duke?" How could my own father allow them to treat me like this?

Little PJ finally emerged from hiding. His face was riddled with guilt. Deep down, he wanted to take up for me. But, in the end, they would have mopped the floor with us both.

I broke the awkward silence first. "So... did you want some ice cream?"

"I'm not hungry anymore," he said, quietly.

"See you tomorrow, Little PJ."

He stopped just before heading out the creamery and said, "Joseph?"

"Yeah?"

"Sorry for making fun of your hat," he said, sheepishly.

Little PJ left before I could respond. I started cleaning off the table and then mopped the floor. Under normal circumstances, I would have felt sorry for myself. But things were different now. I had Meadow in my life. And that joy took away the pain.

"Can I ask you something?" Bridgett Marie said, timidly.

"I'm an open book," I responded.

"Why did your dad treat you like that? He stood by while they harassed you. What kind of father..." she stopped, realizing she might have overstepped her boundaries. "I'm sorry, Mr. Joseph. That was rude," she said.

"Honey, there's nothing to be sorry about. My father and mother lived with some dark secrets. A life of regret was the penalty for their choices. They couldn't forgive themselves, so they punished their only son for their mistakes."

Tears streamed down Bridgett Marie's cheeks as she said, "In a weird way, that makes sense. Forgiving yourself isn't easy. And holding on to the pain..." she couldn't continue. Bridgett Marie buried her face in her hands and sobbed like a child. I didn't patronize her with empty clichés. I put my hand on her shoulder and waited for her to compose herself. Then, I continued my story.

Chapter 4

A Special Assignment

I arrived at O'Dell's at 6:50am. I was so excited to see Meadow that I'd barely slept. I made sure I was a little early. I didn't want to chance missing her. It was nice waiting on her. The fall air was crisp and the leaves were just turning their reds and oranges.

Five minutes passed, and still no Meadow. My thoughts raced. Did she go to school without me? I tried to calm the erratic percolations in my head. But still, I couldn't help looking at my watch every 15 seconds. What was wrong with me?

Suddenly, two hands grabbed me from behind, and a loud "BOO!" was shouted. I yelled at the top of my lungs. I turned and there was Meadow, laughing uncontrollably. She was a sight for sore eyes. She put me into a state of momentary shock, but it was worth it. I had never made a girl laugh like Meadow laughed that morning. It felt good, even if it was at my own expense.

"I got you good, didn't I?" Meadow gloated.

"You sure did," I admitted.

We made small talk on our way to school. Meadow led the conversation off, as usual. As our friendship grew, I would come to realize, this was one of her strengths. She was a go-getter, a natural leader, and she seemed so sure of herself. Her confidence motivated me to be better.

"So, Meadow, there are a lot of things to do around here. What kind of stuff are you into?" I asked.

"Going to the movies or shopping... you know... Normal stuff."

"We don't have any of that here," I said, humbly.

"Don't remind me," she sighed.

"Well, there's Jimmy's souvenir shop. He has some decent stuff."

"Joseph, you are such a country boy." She was right. I was a country boy. I couldn't imagine living in 'the big' city. It had to be exciting. I wondered what brought Meadow and Mrs. Kat to a town like ours. I could tell they just weren't the quiet town type.

"What do you do for fun around here?" she asked.

"Well... there are a lot of things people do for fun. They fish, hunt, swim, go inner-tubing or camping. It depends on the season."

"Joseph, I didn't ask you what 'people' do for fun. I asked what YOU do for fun," Meadow exclaimed.

The question made me canvass the landscape of my life. Up to this point, it hadn't been filled with loads of fun. I wished I could have lied to her. I wanted to tell her hundreds of interesting stories. But I'd lived a boring life. The creamery took up most of my time.

I took a deep breath, and decided to be honest. I confessed, "The shop keeps me pretty busy. Little PJ is my best friend, so we hang out a lot. And, when I have a little down time, I write. Oh, yeah. And I hang out with Sarah, too. She's my second best friend."

"So, how long have you and Sarah been dating?" she queried.

"We don't date. She's just my friend," I answered, defensively.

"Joseph, you have to have a girlfriend. Everyone knows that girls love ice cream and you own an ice-cream shop. You probably have all the girls in town lined up to ask you out," she teased.

I could feel myself blushing again. She had a knack for doing that. I had to play it cool. I didn't want her to know that I hadn't had any luck with the opposite sex.

Confidently, I said, "I'm keeping my options open." I couldn't believe I'd just said that. It didn't even sound like me.

"Really, Joseph? I didn't know you were such a ladies man," she joked.

"I'm not... I mean, I am... I mean... never mind," I blundered.

No matter how awkward or silly I felt, my time with Meadow was a gift. That 40-minute walk whisked by in a moment. Little PJ was standing in front of the school. He wore a devilish grin. Nervously, I waited for him to embarrass me with whatever heinous comment was on his mind.

"Let me get the door for you, Meadow," Little PJ said, gallantly.

"Thank you, Little PJ," she said.

Then, he looked at me, raised his left eyebrow in a questioning manner, and said, "You too, Joseph."

I ignored him and walked through the double doors.

I spent the majority of the morning watching all the guys in class stare at Meadow. I couldn't blame them. I couldn't help staring at her either. Before I knew it, lunch crept up on us. Little PJ, Sarah, Meadow, and I sat together. We must have looked like an odd bunch: the tomboy, two scrubby guys, and the beauty.

We took turns taking out our lunches. Little PJ had his customary peanut butter and jelly sandwich, apple, and milk. I pulled out a ham and cheese sandwich, banana, and candy bar. Little PJ always swapped his apple for something I brought. It was never a fair trade. Sarah left the table to stand in line for a hot lunch. Meadow pulled a bruised pear from her jacket pocket.

This was the second day that Meadow had a pear for lunch. I stared at the battered fruit. It looked like it had been picked up off the side of the road. Yesterday, she said she forgot her lunch in the refrigerator. Today, she didn't bother to make an excuse. It didn't take me long to figure out. Mrs. Kat didn't have enough money to send Meadow to school with a decent lunch.

As she chewed on her fruit, I humbly asked, "Meadow, can you do me a favor?"

"Yeah... What do you need?"

"My mom makes me the same lunch every day. I'm so tired of it. I'd rather eat the food here. She would freak out if I told her I didn't like her food. You could eat my lunches. That way, I'd eat something new each day."

Meadow bowed her head in shame and said, "Joseph... I couldn't."

"It looks like you left your lunch at home again. This way, you don't have to worry about forgetting it. Please take it," I said, as I pushed my lunch in her direction.

Meadow reluctantly grabbed the bag. I took off to the lunch line before she could reconsider. I had no idea how I'd come up with something so creative. Lord knows my mother hadn't made my lunch... well, ever.

Just my luck, they were serving meatloaf, bland mashed potatoes, and corn. I returned to Little PJ's giggles. He knew that I hated meatloaf. But I would choke it down, for her. I found that Meadow was open to the gift of charity, as long as it was respectfully wrapped.

The first bell rang. I scraped my leftover meatloaf into the garbage and stacked my tray. I turned around to the embrace of Meadow. There we were, hugging in the middle of the lunchroom. She whispered in my ear, "Thank you, Joseph." Her words melted me. Her breath was warm and her hair smelled like wildflowers. I made good on my promise. I brought her lunch and choked down horrible cafeteria food the entire year.

Meadow and I headed to O'Dell's after school. Duke's eyes almost popped out of his head. "Who is this?" he asked, surprised.

"This is Meadow. My locker partner," I said, nervously.

She extended her hand and said, "It is nice to meet you, Mr. O'Dell."

"Hello, young lady."

I tried to cut their conversation short.

"Sir, we have a project we really need to get finished before the end of the week. We were planning to work on it between customers – that is, if you don't mind."

"Joseph, don't be ridiculous. Of course you can work on your project between customers, son," he said, sympathetically.

Duke was pouring it on thick. He always did this song and dance when someone new came into the shop. I pulled money out of my tip jar and bought Meadow some pralines n' cream.

"Thank you," she said, gratefully.

"No problem."

"Alright, Joseph, let's get to work. What don't I know about you?" she asked assertively.

"You pretty much know everything about me. The shop... Little PJ... My poetry and Sarah... that's about it."

"What do you write about?"

"I write about a lot of things. It just depends on what I'm inspired by."

"What things inspire you?" she asked, sincerely.

"The thing that inspires me most is my grandfather," I said, without a doubt.

"Does he live around here?"

"No. He died a while back."

"I'm sorry, I didn't know."

"It's ok. He died a long time ago. He loved art. I still have some of his pictures in my room."

"Maybe you could show me."

"Anytime, Meadow," I responded, excitedly.

She took a few moments to jot down notes.

Her brow furrowed before she said, "Joseph, you know what you need?"

"What?" I asked, interested.

"A nickname. Everyone has a nickname where I'm from. I think I'll call you JoJo. It's cute."

I'd never had a nickname. In some, strange way, it made me feel special. "I don't mind if you call me JoJo. Just don't do it around Little PJ. I would never hear the end of it."

"No problem, I will only call you JoJo when it's just us," she said, satisfied.

"Ok." I agreed.

"Well, JoJo, I think I have everything I need. What do you want to know about me?"

"Everything." The answer slipped from my lips. I couldn't believe I'd let that come out of my mouth. It sounded like a bad pickup line.

Meadow answered readily. "Well, like I said in class, my parents are divorced. That is why I'm here. This town is a little boring, but I'm starting to like some things about it. I miss my friends back home. I took ice-skating and ballet classes all my life, but I really didn't like either."

"What do you want to be when you grow up?" I asked.

"I've always wanted to act. I know it sounds crazy, but I do. I want to make it to the big screen someday and mingle with all the beautiful people. Their lives seem so exciting and carefree. I want that," she said with a huge grin.

Meadow and I spent my entire shift talking. She made it easy to be myself.

Little PJ and Sara came in later that evening. They decided to work on their project at O'Dell's, too. Despite the occasional funny face from Little PJ, it was a good night. Before mounting my bike, Meadow said, "Thanks for everything, JoJo. They don't make people like you where I'm from."

Friday came around quickly. Our presentations were due. I could see the jitters on everyone's faces. At that age, it was tough getting up and spilling your guts in front of the entire class. Meadow and I did our presentations last.

"Joseph, you first," Meadow said, after giving me a nudge. I kept my report short and sweet. Stealing a quick glance at Meadow, I began:

It is said that "Beauty" is only skin deep. I couldn't agree more. Real beauty is something we can't see. The true test of beauty is when you meet someone who can make you feel comfortable in your own skin. True beauty is when you can put your guard down and just laugh. Meadow has this. Most of you know that Meadow is new to town. And, it's no secret; she's really pretty. But, what most of you may not know is that she is talented, kind, and the most beautiful person I've ever met.

The class didn't give me much applause. As a matter of fact, I got a few, funny faces from some of the guys. They didn't expect me to be so sensitive. My stomach was calmed down until Mrs. Pittman said, "Ok Meadow, it's your turn." Meadow began:

Moving is always hard. But, sometimes you meet someone that makes it easier. Joseph has been that person for me. Joseph works at O'Dell's Creamery and, in my opinion, is the town's most eligible bachelor. *I mean, what lady doesn't like ice cream? (The class broke out into laughter.)*

But, seriously, Joseph has a heart bigger than this room. No matter where life takes me, I will never forget Joseph O'Dell.

The class clapped for Meadow's presentation, and we retreated to our seats. Mrs. Pittman wiped tears from her cheeks. With a frog stubbornly lodged in her throat, she said, "Please excuse me, class."

After a few moments, she returned, looking more composed. After discussing our reports, she dismissed us for the weekend.

Meadow and I had made an impact that day. And, for a time, we would be inseparable. She gave a simple boy like me a reason to dream.

Chapter 5

Christmas Break

It was Christmas break. The town had transformed into a winter wonderland. The roofs and sidewalks were heavy with freshly packed snow. The storefronts and houses were adorned with wreaths and bright lights. A spirit of hope and thanksgiving covered us like wool sweaters on an icy day. The only complaint I had about the season was the cold.

Sub-zero temperatures were a frequent guest this time of year. The air was so cold and dry that you could cut your nose if you rubbed it wrong. Even so, the frosty elements did not take away from the magic of the time.

Meadow and I had become much closer. We spent all the holidays together. For Halloween, we wore matching pirate costumes and went trick-or-treating with Little PJ and Sarah. My family didn't come together during Thanksgiving, and Mrs. Kat couldn't afford a large meal. So I packed a lunch for Meadow and I. We got lost in one of the local maize fields and had our own reason to be thankful.

Today would weave a tapestry of emotions. It was the first day I visited Meadow's house. Her mom said she wanted to get to know me a little better. Mrs. Kat wanted to give me the "once-over", since I was spending so much time with her daughter. Meadow made it clear that she didn't want me to be there for long. We made plans to go ice-skating on Lonely Lake, after a brief reintroduction to Mrs. Kat.

I worked the early morning shift since school was out. Duke graciously let me take off around 3:00pm. I went straight to Meadow's house. I couldn't ride my bike, because the snow was too deep. The powder was so fresh that it sounded like crunching potato chips.

The air could suck the life out of you if you let it, but I was prepared. I wore my heavy coat, gloves, a red scarf that I had wrapped twice around my neck, and boots. The temperature was a teeth-shattering 19 degrees. But the thought of spending time with Meadow warmed me.

The sight of Meadow's house rattled me. From the looks of it, no one had done any fixes or maintenance to the house for quite some time. The porch was worn and tattered. The fence that surrounded the house was in shambles. The roof, heavy with snow, sagged in the middle. And there was a piece of cardboard where a windowpane should have been. It was held to the frame by duct tape.

I was nervous. I could hardly muster the courage to knock on their door. I really wanted Mrs. Kat to like me. Taking a deep breath, I opened up the rickety gate that was half off its hinges, walked up the uneven stairs, and knocked.

Mrs. Kat answered with booze-soaked breath.

She said, "Come on in, Joseph."

She was wearing a full-sized winter coat, jeans, and boots. I just assumed she was accompanying us to the lake.

I started taking off my boots when Mrs. Kat said, "No, Joseph, you don't need to take off your boots."

"It's OK, Mrs. Kat. I don't want to track mud into your house," I said, naively.

After removing my boots and coat, I realized why she wanted me to keep my gear on. The house was freezing.

Mrs. Kat, sensing my discomfort, said, "I'm sorry for the cold, Joseph. The damn furnace went out this morning."

She'd told a half-truth. The furnace had broken long before that morning. Her worn carpet floor was as hard as a rock. Their old, torn-up sofa was so cold that it was slightly damp. There was a hint of mildew in the air. I could feel it in my gut; they hadn't had heat the entire winter!

Mrs. Kat couldn't afford repairs for the furnace. She could barely afford the bare necessities. The house was cluttered and dark. Liquor bottles occupied most of the counter space, and a dog-eared book was used to level the rickety coffee table. The linoleum in the kitchen was cracked and missing in a few places. The walls were lined with dingy wallpaper that was peeling from most of the seams. Dishes were piled in the sink, and the counters were covered in filth.

Meadow walked out of her room. I could tell from the surprised look on her face she hadn't heard me come in. Meadow seemed uncomfortable. She was probably ashamed of the condition their home was in. She grabbed her skates. Then, she pulled me by the arm and ushered me out the door.

"We'll be back later," she snapped at her mother.

I sat on the porch to put my shoes and coat on. Meadow did not wait for me. She mumbled under her breath as she cascaded down the old stairs and out the fence. I shoved my arms hastily into my coat sleeves. Then, I ran to her. She grumbled, "I can't believe she let him come in... maybe, if we had heat... maybe, if she wasn't drunk all the time... ugh." Her brisk stride turned into a jog.

I yelled, "Meadow!" to which, she didn't respond. I sprinted and grabbed her hand from behind. Again, I uttered softly, "Meadow."

She came to a stop, but I could feel the frustration pooling in her body. She gripped my hand as tight as a vice. We stood there, for a few moments, in silence. Finally, she turned around and gave me that smile I was so accustomed to.

"I'm sorry, JoJo. Let's go skate," she said, sincerely.

"Meadow, are you ok?" I asked, concerned.

"I'll be alright. It's just my mom. She needs to get over my dad. He obviously didn't care enough about us. I got over it, so why can't she? All she does is sit around and drink all day."

"I'm so sorry..." I started, but she cut me off.

"Can we talk about something else?"

We moved on to lighter conversation, as we got closer to our destination.

The lake was like an icy paradise. The snow bordering its shores reflected the sunlight. Naked trees stood guard around us. The frozen water beckoned us to walk across its hazy surface.

She looked at the lake in awe then asked, skeptically, "JoJo, are you sure we can skate on that?"

"Yes, city girl," I teased, and walked onto the lake to prove its integrity.

She called out, "I guess its OK. Give me a minute. I need to lace-up my skates."

Meadow leaned against a large rock at the edge of the frozen water, removed her boots, and put on her skates. I walked back to the snowy shore.

"Aren't you going to skate?" she asked me.

"I don't have any skates."

"Then, what are you going to do?"

"I'm going to watch you," I said, assertively.

"So, basically, you're trying to bore yourself to death," she teased.

"No, not at all," I chuckled. "I haven't written in a while. You skate... I write."

"Suit yourself, JoJo, but you're missing out," she said, playfully.

Meadow attacked the ice, punishing it with the tips of her skates. Her strides were powerful and her turns were aggressive. The friction with her mom motivated this icy routine. Fast, brash, and reckless was the name of the game.

Her intensity increased the longer she was on the ice. She leaped longer and higher, and her spins increased in torque. Her stops should have broken the ice beneath her.

"Meadow!" I finally called out to her.

She stopped immediately. Her fists were clenched and her breaths were labored. It was as if I had woken her from some terrible dream.

I said the first words that came to my heart, "Meadow, let it go. It will be OK, I promise."

She took a few moments to digest my advice, and then nodded her head in agreement. She skated more serenely. She executed moves that took my breath away. This was the first time in my life I paid complete and total attention. Captivated, all I could do was ask myself a series of silly questions. Is this real? Is this all a dream? How did a guy like me get so lucky? It felt like I watched her for hours. I never got around to writing. But that was fine by me.

Eventually, Meadow left the confines of the frozen lake and came back to the shore to change into her boots.

"You are so good," I gushed.

"I started skating when I was three."

"Meadow, you are really, really, good," I repeated.

"You're sweet, JoJo. Are you ready to take me home? I'm beat!"

I walked her home with a heavy heart. She could tell that something was wrong. I wore my heart on my sleeve.

"What's wrong, Joseph?" she asked, concerned.

"Nothing. I'm just tired, too," I lied.

"Ok," she said, doubtfully.

We settled into an uneasy silence as we walked. The idea of her and Mrs. Kat wearing layers of clothes to survive gnawed at me.

"I had a really good time today," Meadow said, with a smile on her face.

"So did I," I said, with an occupied mind.

"You're a good friend, JoJo."

"You make it easy," I said, humbly.

"I better get back and check on my mom. She irritates me, but she's all I got..."

"That's not true," I interrupted.

"What do you mean?" she asked.

"You'll always have me, too," I said, bashfully.

She hugged me and ran for the door.

I called out, "Meadow!"

She turned around and responded, "Yeah?"

I took my scarf off and wrapped it around her neck twice. She embraced me again before going inside.

I arrived home covered in concern. I reached my house and took off my snow gear at the door. I was so distressed that I skipped dinner and headed for bed. Duke noticed me from the living room.

He bellowed, "Your free-loading friend is downstairs. Tell him to bring his own food instead of always eating mine." I sighed, slumped my shoulders, and continued down the stairs.

Little PJ was making himself right at home. He had a comic book in one hand and one of Duke's pork chops in the other. Regardless of Duke's attitude, it was good seeing my best friend. My mind worked overtime as he greeted me. "Your mom let me in. She told me you were out with your girlfriend."

"She did not."

"Well, she didn't TELL me that you were with Meadow. But, if you weren't with me or at the shop, then you had to be out somewhere romancing," he said.

"You sound jealous. C'mon, Little PJ, I would never leave you," I teased.

"Whatever. I'm not jealous. I could have a girl like Meadow if I wanted," he scoffed.

I'd touched a nerve, so I tried to put Little PJ at ease. "Of course you could. You're the man," I said, confidently. He cracked a smile. "I really need your help, Little PJ."

"With what?" he asked, puzzled.

"Counting my life's savings," I said, very matter-of-factly.

"You have a life savings?" he asked, shocked.

"Well, yeah," I admitted.

It was tough for Little PJ to wrap his mind around my money stash. But he didn't understand my relationship with Duke. O'Dell's was the cornerstone of our relationship. He paid me a weekly salary and let me keep my tips. However, he expected me to provide for my own needs. I bought my own clothes, school supplies, and anything else I needed to go about life. Over time, I became very frugal. I saved for the "what if".

I retrieved a rusty coffee-can from the bottom of my nightstand. It was filled with rolled up dollar bills. Then I pulled out an old, 5-gallon paint bucket full of change. I'd cut a slit in the lid to create a makeshift piggy bank. The bucket was almost full. It was so heavy that we had to drag it across the floor. Little PJ's eyes opened as wide as donuts.

"That is a lot of money! What are you going to do with it?"

"I really didn't know, until today. Just help me count it," I said, in a stern tone.

It took us over an hour but we counted all of it.

"I should have just enough," I said, triumphantly.

"Just enough for what? What's going on?" Little PJ asked, skeptically.

"OK, but you have to keep it a secret."

"OK..."

"I should have just enough to help Meadow and her mom. They have gone all winter without a furnace. Did you feel how cold it is out there?" I asked, seriously.

"Yeah... it's freezing."

"Well that's how cold it is in their house. It just isn't right!"

"Are you going to go to Mr. Smith's Stove and Furnace tomorrow?"

"No. I can't just walk in there and buy a furnace. Mr. Smith and Duke are old buddies. He would call Duke and mess up everything."

"So how are you going to do it?"

"I know who can help us," I said, confidently.

Little PJ accompanied me to the shop the next morning. He stayed there my entire shift. We headed to my house around 5pm. Little PJ helped me fill a couple of backpacks up with the coins. Trekking through the snow with heavy backpacks was exhausting. When we arrived outside the church, Papa Pete was shoveling snow. It took a few minutes to explain our dilemma and solicit his help.

"Of course I will help, Joseph. But it is hard for me to see you give up all your money. I could talk to Pastor Paul and see if the church has some funds. We could probably cover the entire thing," he said, hopefully.

"I've saved my money for a long time and I couldn't think of a better way to spend it."

"You are a good man, Joseph. I will make sure Mr. Smith puts a rush on it."

"And one more thing... I don't want them to know it's from me. Thanks, Papa Pete."

"No. Thank you, Joseph, and Merry Christmas."

A couple of days passed since exchanging the money with Papa Pete. I was cleaning off one of the table rounds when and I heard the shop bell ring. My back was to the door.

"Welcome to O'Dell's. I'll be right with you," I said, automatically.

I felt a tap on my shoulder. I turned around into the embrace of Meadow.

She whispered softly, "I know it was you."

Grinning ear to ear, I said, "I have no idea what you're talking about."

"My mom wants to invite you over for Christmas Eve."

"I'll be there!" I answered, immediately.

"Great. Just come around 5 o'clock."

"I'm off in 5 minutes. I can walk you home if you want to wait."

"OK."

I took money out of my pocket and shoved it into the till. I poured her a hot cup of cocoa and scooped up some pralines 'n' cream.

"Thanks JoJo," she said, gratefully.

I watched the joy on her face as she ate. I couldn't help it. I was in love with her.

The snow fell lightly as we walked. The soft flakes kissed our cheeks. We took our time, enjoying each other's company. Foggy breaths accompanied our laughs.

"Is Christmas in Seattle a lot like this?" I asked, trying to make small talk.

"It's nice, but it's not like this, JoJo."

We arrived at Meadow's doorstep too soon. I didn't want our time to end.

Meadow seemed a little uncomfortable. She cleared her throat a couple of times and said, "I don't want you to think I'm rude JoJo. I would invite you in but... This is about the time when my mom gets really drunk. And I really don't want you to see that. Plus, the place is a mess. But I will have it cleaned up by the time you come over tomorrow," she said, with her head bowed in shame.

It was a tender moment. For the first time in my life, someone actually cared about what I thought.

I held her hand and said, "Meadow, when I look at your house I don't see a mess. When I look at your mom I don't see a drunk. And when I see you look shameful, all I can do is ask... why? When I look at you, all I see is beauty and potential. You and your mom are my world. So if you don't get around to cleaning up the mess, well, it's fine by me."

She raised her head and smiled tentatively.

"You should get inside, it's cold," I said.

"OK, JoJo. I'll see you tomorrow."

I arrived the next night at Meadow's home at 5:00pm sharp. Mrs. Kat greeted me at the door. She hugged me so tightly, I could barely breathe, and said, "You did it... You and your church friends... You did it. So, who did you tell there? Who do I need to thank? It doesn't matter. Just come in. Come in, Joseph." Mrs. Kat was ecstatic. She ran around her heated home like a giddy schoolgirl.

I took off my shoes. The soles of my feet met a warm floor. The house was clean and organized. Mrs. Kat escorted me to the couch. She ranted, "Those church folks came by and had the furnace installed. They even dropped off care packages with food and clothes. I'm going to do something special for you, little man. I'm going to bake you a cake."

"Ooh, Mrs. Kat, you don't have to do that."

"Shush, Joseph."

I thought it would be best to give Meadow her present while Mrs. Kat pulled a boxed cake mix out of a gift basket, so I wouldn't draw any more attention to myself than absolutely necessary. I pulled a teddy bear and card from my backpack and called Meadow over.

"Thank you. I already have the perfect name. I'll call him JoJo the bear." She cuddled the stuffed bear like a child. "I have something for you, too!" she exclaimed.

Meadow scampered to her room and brought back a card she'd made. "Thank you," I said, gratefully.

Jeremy Rubin

"Don't open it 'till you get home. I'm not as good with words as you are, so I'd rather you read it later."

I was touched. I had never received a gift. Words could not describe what it meant to me.

I looked around the house and said, "The place looks really good."

With a huge smile, she said, "I'm so glad you like it. I worked all last night on it and cleaned a little more this afternoon."

A large clatter came from the kitchen. Mrs. Kat didn't know her way around a kitchen; the evidence was overwhelming. She pulled out a large mixing bowl and cake pan. They appeared to be her only baking materials. She opened a box of spiced cake mix and poured it into the large mixing bowl. Then, she went to her refrigerator and pulled out a carton of eggs. The carton had only one egg left. Setting it aside, she pulled out a bottle of vegetable oil from her cabinet. She poured the oil into a measuring cup. To her disappointment, there was only half the oil she needed. Coming from a creameries family, I knew that Mrs. Kat did not have enough ingredients to make a respectable cake. I could tell by her body language that she knew it, too.

Mrs. Kat looked over the unfinished business in disgust. With slumped shoulders, she rested her hands on the ends of the table and bowed her head in failure. I wondered how long she would stand there before giving up on her promise. It wouldn't have mattered to me. It's the thought that counts.

A few, uncomfortable moments went by. To my surprise, Mrs. Kat raised her head with a triumphant smile. She scooped out half the cake mix from the bowl, added the single egg, and poured in the remaining oil. She mixed the contents ferociously and poured a paper-thin layer of batter into the cake pan.

As the cake cooked in the oven, Mrs. Kat fussed over it like it was a newborn infant. She checked it repeatedly, and was constantly poking it with toothpicks. She didn't leave the oven's side because the batter was so thin and she didn't want the cake to burn.

She pulled it out of the oven and let it sit on the counter. Once it cooled, she brought a slice over to me. With a single tear rolling down her cheek, she said, "See, Joseph? I told you I'd make you a cake!"

"Wow... That's love, Mr. Joseph."

"Indeed it was," I said, with a smile. "As a matter of fact, it was the greatest gift I ever received."

Bridgett Marie erupted in laughter.

Puzzled, I asked, "What's so funny?"

She chuckled, "Really, Mr. Joseph? You have to be joking. A piece of spice cake? That can't be the best gift you've ever received."

I didn't join her laughter, but I smiled until she composed herself.

"You weren't joking," she said, more seriously.

"No, I wasn't, Bridgett Marie. Most people define a gift's value by a price tag. I hope we evolve beyond that one day. The clearance sales, Black Friday, and the trivialization of holidays can cause us to lose something special. Do you know what that is?"

Bridgett Marie took some time to think before answering. "We lose the meaning behind why we give," she said, confidently.

"Young lady, you are brilliant." I responded with a smile.

"So, why was Mrs. Kat's cake the greatest gift you've been given?" she asked.

"Because it was the first and only time in my life when someone gave me their best."

Chapter 6

Sadie Hawkins

It was spring. Flowers were in bloom, the grass was lush, and the days were mild. There was something in the air, which sounds a little cliché, but it was true. I was looking forward to blue skies and fun. Junior high was coming to end, and I intended to make the most of my time.

The Sadie Hawkins Dance was the talk of the school. Little PJ and Sarah decided to go together. There was no attraction between the two, but Sarah liked to keep things simple. She and Little PJ were friends, and he was available, so, why not?

The Sunday before the dance, I left home early. My mother was working in the garden, and Duke slept in, as usual. I made my way to Meadow's house. We had plans to hang out at the lake.

The water was gorgeous that time of year. Frogs basked on lily pads, dragonflies skipped across the glassy surface, and untamed lavender loosely framed the shores of the lake. Meadow was quiet for most of our trip there. She interrupted our rock skipping session with a very awkward question.

"Do you think we're alone?" she asked, seriously.

Confused, I asked, "What do you mean?"

"Do you believe there is something bigger out there? Maybe a God?" I watched the ripples roll over the lake. I took my time to think. She'd posed such an important question.

"For the longest time, I didn't believe in much of anything. But, lately, things are changing. Maybe there is a God or something out there. But, to be honest, I don't know," I said.

Meadow shook her head and explained, "I have this aunt back home. She went to church all the time. She always prayed before she ate and said 'God bless you' to everyone. And she was the most hateful person I knew." Meadow sat down and crossed her arms. She continued, "I tried to come to her with something really big. Before I could get it out she said 'Go pray about it.' She didn't listen to me. She didn't care."

After a few, uncomfortable moments, I asked, "What's wrong, Meadow?"

"You wanna know what's wrong? I prayed for the same thing, for almost a year. And do you know what happened?"

"What?" I asked, sincerely.

"Nothing! Absolutely nothing!"

"I'm sorry, Meadow." It was a weak response. But it was all I had to offer.

She snapped, "I'm sorry for you, too. Your mom and dad hate you. And you've lived in this stupid town your whole life. So why do you believe there's anything out there? What's changed your mind?"

Her words hurt. I felt a lump pulsing in my throat. I tried pacing back and forth to keep from crying. But it didn't work.

I muttered, "Something happened."

In a frustrated voice, she barked, "What could have possibly happened?"

I answered, "You... You happened, Meadow. Do you know how many times I've thought of running away? I was so close a couple of years ago. But I got to the highway and chickened out. I didn't have much of anything before you showed up."

Meadow sprung to her feet and wrapped her long arms around me. She buried her face in my neck and said, "I'm sorry, JoJo. I shouldn't have said that. I was being stupid. I didn't mean to hurt your feelings." She smiled at me, and I couldn't help but smile back. She grabbed the sides of my face and wiped my tears with her thumbs. Her hands were soft and caring. "I'm such a jerk, JoJo. Let me make it up to you."

"Make it up how?" I asked, interested.

"Let me take you to the dance."

"Maybe," I said, playfully.

"C'mon, JoJo, don't be like that. Are you going to make me beg?"

"OK. I'll go with you. But only because you twisted my arm," I joked.

⚯

"Bridgett Marie, hand me that notebook again. I wrote something I want you to read. She inspired it that day."

Bridgett Marie gave me the old notebook and I flipped through its yellowed pages. "Here it is! It's called, Her Hands."

Bridgett Marie read:

Her hands were God's work, evidence of His favor
Embedded in their perfect design
The color of the skin lining her hands was set apart
It would never embrace another

Hints of its hue can be seen in every good thing
But the grand totality of these tones and complexions
Could only be found in two places
On her body and in the Creator's imagination

The skin on her hands was flawless
Absent of fracture, wrinkle, and fold
Her fingertips had no discriminating marks
For they were unnecessary

Being in her presence cannot be described by the human tongue
There is no language or dialect that can accurately translate
The emotions felt, when drawing near to her

A state of nostalgia - though not totally accurate -
Is the closest depiction of what one would feel
When encountering her

She makes one miss things they had no idea they still longed for
Like the way the air smells before the first fall rains
That scent that brings back a flood of good
memories from season's past

That scent is her presence
Her beauty arrests the senses
It is bewildering, but pleasant, constant, yet ever changing
Like a photograph you viewed in your childhood

Twenty years later, the same portrait has
greater depth and more meaning
And that was her beauty's routine
Changing from moment to moment
Growing in depth and in meaning

The week went by in a blur. Every day was full of expectation for the dance. I asked Duke for Saturday night off. He said dances were silly and work came first. So I brought a change of clothes to the shop and had Little PJ meet me there.

My shift came to an end and I nervously changed in the back. I put on my best button up shirt and slacks. I didn't have a mirror to make sure that I was all put together. My insecurities rose to the top. As I tucked in my shirt and buttoned up my pants, I was plagued with self-doubt.

"Why would she even want to go with a guy like me?" I asked myself.

I walked out of the back room. Little PJ said, "You look really good, Joseph." His compliment was exactly what I needed. It brought a smile to my face.

"Thanks. You don't look too bad yourself," I said, to my old pal.

We walked to Meadow's house. The plan was to pick her up, then meet Sarah at the school. Little PJ could tell I was nervous and tried boosting my confidence.

"Joseph, I don't want to get all mushy on you, but you need to know that you are the best friend... well... you are the best friend that anyone... I mean... you're just the best, Joseph," he stammered. "And, if someone can't see that, well... it's their loss. You need to know that."

"Thanks, Little PJ. You're always going to be my best friend. Always."

Meadow opened the door before we had a chance to knock. Mrs. Kat spouted something from the living room, but the door shut before I could decipher the message.

Meadow looked lovely. She pulled her hair back into a neat bun. She wore the sundress that she had on when she first entered the shop. I was speechless.

"Gentlemen," she said, with mock formality.

Little PJ, being the goofball he always was, turned on his best, British accent, and said, "Milady." Then, he grabbed her right hand, and bowed.

"Meadow, you look really nice," I added.

"Thanks. You look great. You too, Little PJ."

We walked to the school, making silly conversation amongst our-selves. We got there just in time to see Pastor Paul escorting Sarah to the front door. He instructed, "You kids have a good time. Sarah, I will pick you up after the dance, honey."

"OK, daddy," she said, sweetly.

The four of us had a blast that night. For the most part, we loitered around the punch bowl and people-watched. Little PJ entertained us, for hours, doing impressions of our classmates. I hadn't had so much fun in my entire life.

The last song of the night came. Little PJ grabbed Sarah by the hand. He promenaded her through the gym like they were dancing in a royal ballroom. Meadow took my hand and led me to the middle of the dance floor. I was the envy of every guy in our school.

We swayed back and forth and she laid her head on my shoulder. It felt like she was the only thing in the universe. The last song came to an end, and I reluctantly let her go. We all clapped and made our way out of the gym.

Pastor Paul was right outside to meet us. "You kids have fun?" he asked.

"Yes, Pastor Paul," we answered, in unison.

After he left with Sarah, Little PJ and I walked Meadow home. It was a beautiful, starry night. The air was the perfect temperature. Meadow grabbed my right arm, and Little PJ strolled along on my left side. Life couldn't get any better than this.

A block from Meadow's house, Little PJ said, "You guys go ahead. I need to tie my shoes." He was a good wingman.

"I had such a good time with you," I said, nervously.

"I had a good time with you, too, JoJo. Little PJ is such a nut. He had me laughing all night."

"Me too. I hope I'm not getting you home too late."

"Don't worry about it. My mom is probably passed out already."

"Good. I don't want to get on Mrs. Kat's bad side," I joked, trying to keep things light.

"Trust me, you could never do anything to get on her bad side."

When we reached her porch, the situation got a little uneasy for me. I didn't know what to do next.

"Goodnight, Meadow," I said, as my palms began to sweat.

"Good night, JoJo."

We stood there for a few, awkward moments before I retreated down the steps.

Upon reaching the bottom step, I heard Meadow call out, "JoJo!"

Meadow bounded down the stairs and kissed me on the cheek. I almost fainted.

I played it cool until she went inside. As soon as the door shut, I threw up my hands and ran down the block to Little PJ. I hugged him and spun him around.

"You got a smooch, didn't you?" he asked.

"Little PJ," I replied, in the savviest tone I could muster, "a gentleman never tells."

"Well, spill the beans then," he said, obnoxiously.

I laughed with my friend. I walked home with a new confidence. For at least one night, Joseph O'Dell was a king.

"Love like that doesn't exist anymore," Bridgett Marie said, sadly.

"What do you mean?" I asked.

"People aren't innocent and love isn't simple. Maybe it was back in your day. Things like real love and happily ever after are for the movies. As soon as you open up and trust someone... never mind. You wouldn't understand."

"Bridgett Marie, I understand more than you know. People have been the same for a long time. We are full of potential. Some of us chase after our dreams, but most don't have the courage for the journey. If you think this is going to be the typical 'boy meets girl' story, you're mistaken. Little lady, forget all the romantic comedies you've watched and fairy tales you've read. The road to happily ever after is full of obstacles, disappointments, and tears. If you have the courage to persevere to the end, you will be greatly rewarded. Your prize will be a regretless life, a full heart, and eternal peace."

Bridgett Marie asked, "What do true love and dreams have to do with each other? They seem like two separate issues."

"The two are closer than you think. Dreams and love need each other."

"I don't understand," she said, puzzled.

"You can't truly love someone without establishing your own self-worth. Self-worth comes from chasing the things we are passionate about – our dreams. A man without a dream is lost. Lost men don't know how to love. Find yourself through the power of your own dreams. And you will have your happily ever after, too."

"I'll believe it when I see it," she said, before rolling her eyes and pursing her lips.

Chapter 7

A Summer to Remember

It was a scorching, summer day and O'Dell's was packed over capacity. It seemed like hundreds of orders were being called in at the same time. Tourists, travelers, and locals all rushed in. Duke and I were doing our best to keep up, but it was tough. The only redeeming side to this chaos was the amount of money I made. The summer season made up for every slow spot during the rest of the year.

The mob of customers could be overwhelming. But Duke and I had a system. Duke stayed at the counter and handled all the to-go orders. I welcomed the customers coming through the door, served all the people eating in, and bussed the tables.

I was focused. I disconnected myself from the masses and honed in on each, individual order, one at a time. Our system would have worked more smoothly if we'd hired an extra person for the season. However, Duke was convinced this was a two-man operation. That was how his father had done it, and that was how he intended to do it. The shop bell rang out of control and I hung on for the ride.

This was the time when I truly despised the shop. Customers waltzed in with their lake water soaked swimming trunks and tan lines. Their joy was overwhelmingly evident. I eavesdropped on their conversations of summer fun. I envied them. I wanted to live their lives.

I worked like a dog from sunup to sundown. Duke could not deny my value this time of year. But, true to his nature, he never let me know that he appreciated my good work, no matter how busy we got.

The clock inched toward 4pm. This was the time of day when my favorite visitors showed up. Meadow and Little PJ walked in with waves and smiles. I hollered, "Give me a sec. I have a few more tables to bus." They took a seat at a booth a couple of seats from the door. They were waiting for their daily treat, complements of yours truly.

The two of them made small talk while I cleaned up a couple of tables on the far right end of the shop. There had been a large family occupying the entire section. They were headed to the Grand Canyon. The kids made a huge mess. But the large tip their parents left sparked my forgiveness.

For Meadow, I scooped up some pralines 'n' cream, and I placed rocky road in a waffle cone for Little PJ. The shop traffic died down, so I took a break and sat with my friends. Duke didn't mind, as long as the timing made sense.

"So, how's the ice cream, Meadow?" We were interrupted before Meadow could answer. It was the sound of Logan Stone's car. The engine's rumble rattled the windows of the shop. I immediately scurried behind the counter with Duke.

A gut-wrenching fear came over me. Logan had never been in the shop at the same time as Meadow. He worked out with a special trainer in Seattle the entire summer. He would make me look stupid. I just knew it. Today would be the day that Meadow lost all respect for me; at least, that's what I kept telling myself.

Logan and Big Mike entered the shop, but something was different about them. "Hey, buddy. How is your day going?" Logan said, cordially. He was up to something... but what?

I immediately looked at Meadow. She was staring at Logan like a kid in a candy store. And why wouldn't she? I started to put two and two together. Logan must have seen Meadow though the windows of the shop. And now he was putting on his best "good guy" act.

"I'm doing fine. What can I get you guys?"

"We want two chocolate shakes to go," he said, with a smile.

"Coming right up."

Logan and Big Mike headed off towards Meadow and Little PJ. Big Mike signaled for Little PJ to get out of the booth, while Logan sat beside Meadow. I couldn't hear what they were saying. But her body language was speaking loud and clear. She was definitely interested. He was smiling, she was giggling, and I wanted to throw up.

"Two chocolate shakes!" I said, loudly, trying my best to interrupt them. Logan whispered something into Meadow's ear before retrieving the milkshakes.

He and Big Mike left the shop. I couldn't have been more relieved. I felt a little unsettled about Logan meeting Meadow. What words could they have exchanged?

I walked over to the booth. Little PJ had already made his way back. I tried to remain as cool as possible because I didn't want to come across as jealous.

"So, you met Logan Stone?" I said, nonchalantly.

With a smile on her face, she replied, "Yeah."

Little PJ sensed that this conversation might get a little heavy, so he excused himself. He assured me that we would catch-up later.

I could tell Meadow was impressed with Logan. Her dreamy demeanor amplified my insecurities. "So, what did you guys talk about?" I asked.

"Well... he asked me if I was new to town and he was surprised he hadn't run into me before. He said that he goes to Windham High School. Isn't that where we're going this year?"

"Yes," I reluctantly admitted.

"He said I should try out for cheerleading. Logan thought I'd be a natural. He said that, when I make the squad, I better cheer for him. He's so funny."

"He's a funny guy, alright," I said, facetiously.

"Did you know that he's their star quarterback?"

"You guys sure spoke about a lot."

"Oh, JoJo, you're jealous aren't you? Don't worry, you will always be my best friend."

Great, I thought, to myself. I'll always be in the 'friend zone'. This was getting worse by the minute. It was time to change the subject.

"Meadow, I want to do something different with you tomorrow."

"Like what?"

"It's a surprise."

"What kind of Surprise?"

"I can't tell you. I've already said too much."

"Are you trying to take me on a date?" she asked.

"No! I mean..." I stumbled.

She interrupted, "I'm just joking, JoJo. What time are you picking me up?"

"About 10:00AM."

"OK," she agreed.

After finishing her ice cream, Meadow left the shop. I finished up my shift and went home. My emotions were all over the place.

I picked Meadow up the next morning.

"I know this place. It's about an hour and a half walk from here. Are you up for it?" I asked.

"Let's go," she said, confidently.

We walked along the countryside for several miles. The land was fresh and fertile. Pollen filled the dry air. We scuttled down a few, unpaved roads until we reached some hilly terrain. The road forked at its end. But, just before the fork, lay a trail. The raggedy trail veered off to the right and up an embankment. Thick shrubbery guarded the trail, along with a gate and a sign that read, "Private Property. No Trespassing."

"Where are we?" she asked.

"It's a special place... just follow me."

We climbed over the gate and scaled the steep hill. The dirt was very loose and the rocks were coarse and undependable. This made for a difficult climb. It took us a good 20 minutes to reach the hill's summit.

"Wow, look at this view," she sighed.

The top of the hill opened up to a green pasture with a panoramic view. The pasture itself was only maintained by nature. Wildflowers and tall grass ruled over the land. We could see for miles in any direction. The town, the vineyards, everything looked better from up there.

"Follow me," I said.

I grabbed her by the hand and led her to a large stone about 30 yards away from where we were standing.

"What is this?" she asked. She was referring to a folding chair that leaned against the boulder. A tombstone lay directly in front of the chair.

"It's my grandfather's grave. When he wasn't painting in the basement, he would sit in this very spot, and paint. Grandpa Joe liked the land so much, that he bought as much as he could afford. He asked my father to bury him here when the time came. I followed Duke here one day. He kneeled next to the grave, and cried for hours. I come here from time to time. But you are the first person I've brought with me."

I offered the folding chair to Meadow. We sat there in silence for a moment to take it all in. She broke the silence by saying, "That's odd. Your grandfather's tombstone doesn't have the date he was born or the date he died."

She was right. I had never questioned why my grandfather didn't have the dates he occupied this earth on his tombstone. I had always been more intrigued by its words. It read:

Joseph O'Dell Still Lives

"I'm not sure why there is no date. Sometimes it really does feel like he's still here," I said, proudly.

"Thank you for bringing me here."

"Anytime."

"JoJo, can you promise me one thing?"

"Anything," I said, confidently.

"Don't let high school change you. I'm not saying you can't make new friends. Just don't stop being my friend, OK? I don't know what I'm trying to say... umm... just don't change, JoJo."

"I will always be there for you. No matter what," I vowed.

We stayed there until sunset.

I didn't know it then, but high school was going to change everyone around me, especially Meadow. I would see every demon she was running from. And I was not prepared to fight them all.

Chapter 8

High School

I woke up to a stomachache. It wasn't food poisoning or the flu. This ache was all nerves. It was my first day of high school and I didn't know what to expect. I got dressed in a hurry, skipped breakfast, and made my way to the shop. I was lucky, there were three bus stops in our town and one was right outside O'Dell's. I had a lot on my mind that morning. I asked myself some very tough questions. How was I going to fit in? Would Logan and Big Mike bully me every day? Would my friends stay by my side or would they change? At a certain point, I finally decided to block out all the insecurities and just try to enjoy the moment.

I waited with a few other kids from the neighborhood. Some of them jokingly asked me to go in and get them a sundae. They made me laugh, which felt good to my heart and cut the tension some. I thought, maybe this day wouldn't be half bad. I smiled as the big yellow bus pulled up. I knew it was holding some of my favorite cargo.

Little PJ and Meadow were sitting a few rows back on opposite sides of the bus. They both waved for me to sit with them. I had a tough choice. Would I sit with my lifelong friend or with Meadow? They'd wagered on where I would sit.

Meadow won the bet.

"I saved you a seat," she said, smiling.

"Thanks."

"I'm excited and nervous at the same time," she said, cheerfully.

"Me too," I agreed.

"Is there something wrong? You're being so short with me, JoJo."

"No, I'm OK. I'm just a little nervous. But I'll be OK."

"You're going to be fine. Remember, you have us. Joseph, whatever you do, promise you won't leave me today. Well, unless we have separate classes or something."

I grabbed her hand and said, "I won't. I promise."

The bus pulled in front of Marcus Windham high school. The scene was epic. It looked more like a festival than a high school campus. Students lumped together into three categories: the popular, the involved, and the lost.

The popular students were made up of jocks, cheerleaders, and the beautiful people. Logan Stone was definitely a part of this crew, if not the chairman. These students typically hung out in the parking lot before school. They had muscle cars for transportation. These trendsetters wouldn't be caught dead riding the bus or hanging out with a guy like me.

The second group was known as the involved students. They were academically sound with extracurricular resumes that were second to none. These overzealous volunteers occupied tables lining the walkways. Each table had displays that showcased what made their club interesting and unique.

The last group of students was categorized as the lost. The lost were the newly arrived, sophomore class. We were the people that looked bewildered and amazed. These coeds weren't popular or involved, just stuck in-between.

The thoughts I fought off earlier came rushing back. I was about to walk down the same hallways my father had walked. He was a legend in this place. I could only wonder what kind of mark I would leave.

Sarah and Little PJ marched off the bus behind Meadow and me. But, before our merry group could take it all in, we were interrupted by obnoxious shouting.

"MEADOW!!!"

Who would be calling her name? Who could have known her? OH NO! It was Logan Stone yelling and waving for her to join him in the parking lot. She was being officially invited to loiter around his car with the rest of the "beautiful people."

When Meadow looked back, I knew it was over. She wore a smile bigger than I had ever seen. It was the grin of acceptance.

She said, "Hey Joseph, I'll catch up with you guys later."

In my heart, I knew that I had lost her – at least for the moment. Meadow was no longer a part of the lost student population. The popular side had chosen her, and chosen her early.

I watched as Stone introduced her to everyone. By virtue of his endorsement, she was "in." I had to admit, she looked so happy. Part of me couldn't blame her. I was consistent, dependable, and considerate. But those qualities, however noble, weren't important to most girls her age. They cared about looks, popularity, and status. Who was I kidding? She was out of my league from the start. Why had I convinced myself of the opposite? I swallowed the bitter pill of defeat and headed off into the building.

My first class was math, which wasn't my favorite subject. I was born to be a writer, not an accountant. I would have had a horrible time in the class if it weren't for the instructor, Mr. Burmester. "Burm", as he was known, was well liked. He wore multiple hats at Windham. On top of being the math teacher, he was the athletic director and the advisor for student leadership. He was in great physical shape for his age. His classic slogan was, "Every day is a great day at Marcus Windham high school." And Burm did everything in his power to make sure that that was a fact for all of his students, even me.

Lunchtime came around and the place was a zoo. I was excited to catch-up with the rest of the gang. I didn't have any classes with Little PJ, Sarah, or Meadow. I walked aimlessly through the table rounds that made up our lunchroom until I heard, "Joseph... over here... Joseph... Joseph... right here." It was the voice of Little PJ, and it was music to my ears. He and Sarah had found a spot near the back of the lunchroom, away from the crowds.

Little PJ started in as I sat down. "Joseph, this place is huge. Do you like your classes?"

"Yeah, for the most part. Have you guys seen Meadow?"

"I haven't seen her all day," Sarah responded. "She'll show up, Joseph."

Little PJ cut back in. "Joseph, let's just enjoy ourselves, buddy. We finally made it to high school. We need to live it up."

He always had a way of bringing things back to a positive place. I scanned the area one last time before I bit into my sandwich.

There she was, sitting in the middle of the lunchroom, perched so close to Logan it made me feel sick. I didn't alert Little PJ or Sarah. I didn't want to hear the barrage of insults they would throw at her to protect me.

I stared at Meadow as she laughed and ate with Logan, Big Mike, and a host of others. Just as I was about to break my gaze, Meadow looked right in my direction. I could tell that she was caught off guard.

Our eyes locked.

The initial warmth in her eyes was quickly replaced by guilt and shame. She turned her body and her attention back to Logan and his friends. I guess it was official; our relationship had changed.

Meadow never got on the bus that afternoon. Actually, she never rode the bus again. I wore my depression like a heavy, wet blanket. I sat on the brown leather seats with my head resting against the glass window. Little PJ and Sarah were nice enough not to bring up the subject of Meadow.

We came to Sarah's stop first. Before getting off the bus, she came over to my seat and hugged me. Her show of affection came out of the blue. It was a balm for my wounded heart.

My stop came up next. Little PJ needed to get home. He already had homework. I admired his commitment and told him that I would catch-up with him tomorrow.

I entered O'Dell's and was immediately cornered by Duke. "So, did you see all my awards, Joseph? It probably made you proud to see what your old man has accomplished, huh?" he gloated. I was in no mood for his pompous attitude.

"I didn't see any of your trophies," I said, with more insolence in my voice than Duke was willing to deal with.

"What? Didn't make any friends today?" he sneered. "Big surprise. You need to leave that attitude at the door. Go get changed now!" he yelled.

I headed to the back to put on my ridiculous uniform. When I emerged, Duke said, "I'll be in the back. Here is a list of things for you to do before your shift is over."

"Yes, Sir," I said, respectfully.

Duke had put a few extra things on my to-do list. I didn't mind. Maybe drowning myself in work would get my mind off Meadow.

The day was pretty steady. I was able to tend to my customers and tackle my to-do list. Suddenly, the shop bell rang. It was Papa Pete.

"Hi, Joseph," he greeted me, cheerfully.

"Hi, Papa Pete."

"How was your first day of high school?"

"It was OK, I guess. What can I get you?"

"Actually, I just stopped by to see you. I was just over at Pastor Paul's house. Sarah said you had a rough day and that I should check on you."

"I'm fine."

"Is it about Meadow? I've been meaning to ask you about her. I've seen you two spend a lot of time together. And you've been really gracious with her family..."

"Please, Papa Pete," I interrupted, insisting, "I'm fine," with less patience than before.

"Joseph, I just don't want you to get hurt. That's all," he said, sincerely.

I spoke through pain when I asked, "Why do you care if I get hurt?"

"You remind me of myself when I was younger. You have such a huge heart and you are an amazingly caring person. But there's one thing you need to remember, and it's something that I struggle with myself. You can't save everyone. Sometimes, people have to learn on their own. And just because they don't get it now, doesn't mean they will never get it. Continue to be yourself regardless of how others react. In time, it will all work out for the best. Do you understand?"

"I think so. Sorry for being rude earlier. I'm just having a rough day."

"Don't worry about it. Talk to you later, Joseph."

"Bye, Papa Pete."

A couple of weeks went by and I barely saw Meadow. I would be lying if I said I wasn't upset. It was a Thursday night and I had to handle the shop on my own. Duke was really sick. He was a prideful man. So, leaving the shop in my hands was a big deal. Little PJ spent the entire day with me. I could always count on him.

The night was winding down. We hadn't seen a customer in hours. Suddenly, the all too familiar sound of Logan's Chevy resonated from outside. Logan wanted to ruin my night, once again.

Meadow and Logan entered together. My heart sank. It felt like a punch in the gut.

They made themselves comfortable in one of our booths. She was practically sitting on his lap. What was he thinking? He was almost 19, and she was barely 15. I felt sick. I walked over to the booth to take their order. Meadow didn't even acknowledge me.

"Joseph, get us two root beer floats," said Logan, far more cordially than usual. He was probably trying to impress her.

"Coming right up," I said, woodenly.

I made the floats, but I knew that Meadow didn't like root beer. Logan would have known that if he'd bothered to ask her. I decided to make Meadow her customary pralines 'n' cream. I set the floats in front of Logan. Then, I placed the ice cream in front of Meadow.

"I didn't order that ice cream," Logan snapped.

"It's for Meadow. It's her favorite and there's no charge."

Meadow bowed her head shamefully.

In a condescending manner, Logan said, "Ooh isn't that so sweet. Aren't you just so thoughtful?"

Meadow pushed the bowl of ice cream away. It hurt. She grabbed Logan by the arm and said, "Why don't we just go, Logan?"

"But, what about our floats?" he protested.

"Forget the floats," she said, flirtatiously.

"You're right. Forget the floats."

The power couple left the shop all too quickly.

"Will you spend the night at my house tonight? I mean, only if you don't have anything else going on," I asked Little PJ, humbly.

"I'd come even if I had other plans," Little PJ assured me.

We joked around for most of the night. My emotions ran the gamut from depression to joy and back again. But, overall, Little PJ made me feel a lot better.

A couple of wintery weeks passed. I hadn't seen Meadow at school. She and Logan hadn't wandered their way back into O'Dell's either.

It was a Saturday night and I couldn't sleep. Regardless of how I felt about her relationship with Logan, it bothered me that we weren't friends. It was approaching 10:30pm. I decided that I would sneak out of my house and ride over to Meadow's. I wanted her to know that I wanted her in my life, no matter what.

Rain fell as I biked to her house. I sped up my peddling, hoping I wouldn't be soaked by the time I got there. I got a block away from Meadow's and skidded to an abrupt halt.

Logan's car was parked out front. I figured he was visiting. But I wondered why he had parked so far away. As I walked my bike closer, I realized what was actually happening, though it was almost incomprehensible to me.

Meadow's beautiful hands were pressed against the foggy windows of Logan's car. The car's suspension rocked as the vehicle stood parked. Meadow and Logan were having sex in his back seat.

I turned and vomited on the wet concrete. My mind tried to compute what was going on. I didn't want to believe it. I couldn't watch. I needed to leave. I had never experienced pain like that before.

Unsteadily, I got back on my bike and rode back home. I snuck back through the front door and tiptoed down the stairs. I sat down at my grandfather's desk, drenched from head to toe. I cried myself to sleep.

I woke up around 5:00am, and wrote about the experience. I titled it: *Girl in the Back Seat.*

∞

"Mr. Joseph, she put you through some real pain. I bet you didn't want to talk to her again."

"Quite the contrary, Bridgett Marie, I wanted to understand why she changed."

"What's there to understand?" she asked, passionately. "She up and left you for a jerk. And after everything you did for her, she deserved to be written off."

"Is that what you think?" I asked, tenderly.

She shouted, "Yes, of course it is! People get what they deserve!" She placed her hand over her mouth and sobbed.

In a soft voice, I asked, "What was his name?"

"What was whose name?" she asked, through her tears.

"The man that hurt you," I said, graciously.

"What makes you think I'm hurt? I can't have an opinion?"

I leaned over and wiped the tears beneath her eyes. Her cheeks were warm and flush.

"Hurt people pass judgment so easily," I continued. "Their pain clouds the virtues that make us human. To love... to forgive... to exercise grace... these honorable attributes are lost in their sadness. The truth is that life offers more wonder than any one person deserves, hurt or not."

Bridgett Marie muttered, "Can we switch the subject Mr. Joseph?"

"Of course we can, honey."

Chapter 9

Brave Little PJ

By the heart of winter, Logan Stone was the talk of the town. He and the rest of the Windham Falcons dominated every team they faced. Stone was putting up record-breaking numbers every week. His performance brought national attention to our small town. To say that Logan's popularity was astounding would be an understatement.

Windham would play for the state championship in a couple of weeks. As the star quarterback, Logan was featured in all the regional newspapers. He was recruited by every major football program across the country. Shop owners in our town posted pictures of him on their storefronts. O'Dell's was no exception. I was forced to look at his ugly mug every day. It reminded me of what I had lost. To add insult to injury, Duke wouldn't stop talking about Logan's success.

Meadow's popularity was in sync with Logan's. They were officially an item. She took her job as 'Girlfriend of Logan Stone' very seriously and worked to do everything right. She joined the cheer squad and made captain as a sophomore, which was virtually unheard of. She started wearing makeup, her hair was always flawless, and even her wardrobe changed. She had all the nicest clothes. I was sure Logan bought them for her. I knew Mrs. Kat couldn't afford it.

I bumped into Meadow in the hallways from time to time, but she ignored me. I convinced myself that she was trying to protect me from Logan and his buddies. But there were days when I was more realistic. I just needed to get over it. Obviously, our past didn't mean anything to her. It felt like a cruel joke. Still, a large part of me wanted Meadow to be happy at any cost.

Word was going around town that all of the attention was starting to go to Logan's head. The rumor was that he was taking an interest in other girls. I knew Stone was a ladies' man, but he would be a fool to leave Meadow.

It was late, Wednesday night. At O'Dell's, Papa Pete had just finished up with his youth group. Little PJ kindly stayed and helped me clean up. Duke had left the shop a couple of hours early, so we took on the closing tasks by ourselves. We were just about to turn off the lights when the bell on the door jangled.

Logan, Big Mike, and six of their teammates rumbled in. Little PJ retreated to a booth in the far corner of the shop. I mentally kicked myself. It was my fault that they came in at all. We had been closed for over 10 minutes, but I hadn't yet flipped the "Open" sign to the "Closed" side.

"Sorry guys, we are just closing up. But I can get you something if it's really quick," I said, politely.

Big Mike barked, "You can go when I say you can go. Don't rush us, water girl."

They sat down and talked amongst each other. Reluctantly, I walked over to their booths. They were talking about Meadow.

"So, when are you gonna give Meadow the boot?" Big Mike asked. "Where you're going, there are going to be so many chicks, you won't have time to keep up."

"She's just something to keep me occupied, for now," Logan scoffed. "She's made-up trailer trash," he continued. They all laughed and banged on the table. Logan stood up and, with all the arrogance he could muster, mockingly said, "Could you guys imagine me – The Stone – keeping a girl like her? Yeah right!"

They all continued to laugh.

"Don't talk about her like that!" I snapped.

I knew it was a mistake as soon as it left my lips. I was surprised that I had displayed such nerve, especially being so outnumbered. But, despite the distance between us, Meadow meant everything to me.

Big Mike stood up and faced me belligerently. "What did you say?" he yelled.

Before Mike could punish me, Logan stepped in front of him and said, "I'll handle this, big guy."

Logan got within a couple inches of me. He looked me up and down a few times. The room was totally quiet.

"Ooh, that's right. You have a crush on the trailer trash. Don't you? DON'T YOU?"

"She is... I mean was... my friend, Logan. I just don't think you should talk about her like that," I said, nervously. Logan laughed and pointed at me. The rest of his teammates followed suit.

"That's right, water girl. She used you until she found something better. That's the difference between guys like me and guys like you. Guys like you never get what they want. Me, on the other hand, well there's nothing I can't have. And when I'm done, I move on to the next project."

My face was flushed and tears welled up in my eyes. They rolled down my cheeks and I began to sniffle.

"Is the water girl crying?" Logan asked, teasing me. He slapped my hat off my head. By then, I was crying uncontrollably. Big Mike decided that it was time for him to join in the fun. He started poking me in my chest. His huge index finger hurt my boney sternum. It wasn't long before the entire team joined in.

Big Mike chanted in a whinny voice, "Look at the water girl, crying! Look at the water girl, crying!"

I didn't fight back. I tried to wait out the torment. I just wanted it all to end.

Out of nowhere, Little PJ leapt between the mob and me. He was holding a mop that had been standing against the wall beside him. He yelled, "Get back! Back away from Joseph!" I think his shrill voice startled them more than anything else. Little PJ stood there shivering from fear. But he held the mop like a Bo-staff and stood his ground. His entire body turned red from the stress and tears began to roll from his cheeks, too. "GET OUT OF HERE! GO! JUST GO!" he commanded.

They laughed at us before Logan said, "It doesn't matter. You two aren't worth it. Let's go, guys."

I locked the door behind them. Little PJ and I cleaned up the shop in silence.

After a few moments, I said, "Little PJ... I just want to say..."

"It's Ok, Joseph," he interrupted. "I should have been there for you last time. Sorry for not sticking up for you before."

I thought about Papa Pete's words while I mopped the floor. He'd spoken earlier that night about the importance of service. He'd challenged everyone to identify someone who needs help, and to do something to make that person's life easier. His point had been that, no matter how bad things get for us, someone else always has it worse. And serving those people keeps us from feeling sorry for ourselves.

I thought to myself, "Who has it worse than me? Who can I help?" Duke had the shop, my mother had her garden, Little PJ had me, and Meadow... well, she could have whom or whatever she wanted.

As I thought it over, my mind kept coming back to Meadow's mom. Mrs. Kat didn't have anyone. She was stuck in a rundown house, her husband left her with nothing, and her daughter had gone off the deep end. The only thing she had to comfort her was the bottle. In that moment, I decided I would help Mrs. Kat.

The state championship was creeping up on the town. It was the only thing the customers talked about. I tried my best not to listen to the chatter, but it was impossible to avoid.

One Monday, I stumbled onto a conversation that I wished I'd never heard. I was busy bussing a table while a group of girls conversed in a booth next to me. They were so deep in gossip that they didn't notice my presence.

"You know, Meadow slept with Big Mike? How could she? She knows that he and Logan are best friends."

Another girl in the group gaggled, "I heard she's having sex with the entire team. I hope the little hussy doesn't ruin our shot at state."

I wished I hadn't overheard them. Whether the rumors were true or not, Meadow had become "that girl."

Later that evening, my mother and I crossed paths. I was heading through the kitchen to my room. I so desperately wished that we were closer.

Reaching out for some connection, I tentatively asked, "Mom, do you mind if we talk about something?"

"I'm tired. Talk to Duke," she said, coldly. She headed to her room. I forced myself to accept that my mother wasn't emotionally available. I swallowed my pride and retired to my quarters.

Game day came in no time, and the entire town shut down. Almost everyone commuted to Seattle to watch the state championship. Even Sarah and Little PJ joined in the festivities. I convinced Duke to let me stay and keep the shop open. I explained we would be the only store open to travelers, so our profits would go through the roof. Duke wasn't one to argue with a good business decision. He let me man the store by myself while he and the rest of the town enjoyed the game.

That Saturday was the longest Saturday of my life. I deep-cleaned the shop and completed all my homework with time to spare. Still, the shop was empty. Eventually, I brought out the notebook that held my poetry. I flipped through the pages and reminisced on some of my previous work. It was an hour before closing, and I was lost in my thoughts.

"RING... RING... RING..." The shop bell startled me. I looked up. It was her. I was amazed and nervous at the same time. Leaving my notebook on the counter, I scooped up some pralines 'n' cream. I placed the ice cream down at a booth and said, "Hi Meadow."

"Joseph, I can't take this," she said, sheepishly.

"Sure you can." After she hesitantly sampled the ice cream, I asked, "Why aren't you at the game, cheering?"

"I dropped the cheer squad a few days ago. It was lame."

"I thought you'd at least go to watch Logan."

"We broke up. Speaking of that, are people talking about me?"

"Umm..."

"That's OK," she interrupted. "You don't have to tell me. I know they are."

"Well, they are saying some things. But I don't believe any of it," I said, with conviction.

"Just so you know, Joseph... some of it is probably true. I did sleep with Big Mike."

"But why, Meadow? You don't have to do any of this. You are so much better than this."

She lost her temper and yelled, "DON'T JUDGE ME! DON'T YOU DARE JUDGE ME, JOSEPH! Logan was just using me. I heard what he was saying about me... the names he was calling me. I was just a joke to him and his friends. So, I had sex with Big Mike to get back at him. Now he knows how it feels to be used. He deserved it."

She was only 15 years old, but she spoke like a woman twice her age. I decided that it might be best to change the subject. "How is your mother?" I asked.

"She stays in the house. She drinks. She hasn't changed," she said, very matter-of-factly.

"I'm sorry to hear that."

"Just so you know, you won't be seeing me around much anymore. This town is too slow for me. I have friends in Seattle... friends in Spokane. They know how to have a good time."

"Are you moving away?"

"No. But I'm getting out of this hellhole every chance I get."

"I'm not sure what to say," I muttered.

She got up from the booth and said, "Thanks for the ice cream."

"Things will get better, Meadow," I reassured her.

"Sure they will," she said, sarcastically. She pulled some money out of her pocket and headed for the cash register.

"You know you don't have to pay. It's on me."

"No, Joseph, I'm not accepting any more charity," she said, sternly.

My notepad caught her attention.

"You're still at the poetry, huh?"

"Yeah... I guess you could say that."

She turned a couple of pages and said, "What is this?" She pointed at the title at the top of the page: *Girl in the Back Seat*.

"Uhh... I just... uhh..."

I snapped the book shut and stumbled over my words. I had no response.

"You saw us, didn't you? Didn't you?" she interrogated.

"Yes, Meadow. But it's not what you think. I wasn't spying on you. I rode to your house to talk. I wanted to be friends whether you were with Logan or not. I didn't want to see you guys doing *that*."

"Well, read it," she instructed.

"I shouldn't," I protested.

"It is about me. You didn't ask my permission to write it. So read it," she insisted.

"I don't need to read it. I have it memorized."

"Well then, recite it, genius. I'm really interested to see how your opinion of me has changed," she said, in a condescending tone.

"OK, Meadow."

I gazed into her eyes and spoke:

> *Pretty hands press against cold glass*
> *And separate the window's fog*
> *I want to run away from this gut-wrenching scene*
> *Paralyzed, my feet stuck in the mud and bog*
>
> *She gave something precious away,*
> *In exchange for a passing thrill*
> *Beautiful girl, you're priceless*
> *Why settle for the short end of the deal*
>
> *Scrunched and contorted in the crevasse of his back seat*
> *You jade your body, mind, and soul with every passing heartbeat*
> *The act is over and done with; don't go back, you have a choice*
> *There's a grace that will mend you and in that love you can rejoice*
>
> *You were created to sit in the front*
> *To be placed on pedestals as high as the sky*
> *God has given you wings*
> *Beautiful girl, pick them up and fly*
>
> *You are the head, not the tail*
> *Part of a plan, not a by-product of a mistake*

Realize your purpose, don't sell yourself short
It makes my heart ache

Lovely, I don't see you for what you have done
But for whom you were always intended to be
Beautiful girl, I can say without a doubt
You are not the girl in the back seat

She looked at me with a perplexed gaze. She didn't expect to hear grace in my words. She had a tough time receiving it. I was not moved by the rumors, and I couldn't care less about her mistakes. She looked down at the floor in shame, shook her head a few times, and turned to exit O'Dell's.

"Bye, Joseph," she said, softly.

I called after her, "Have faith... I will wait on you."

She looked at me through the other side of the glass. I could tell that she had heard me.

She opened the door and asked, "What did you say?"

With conviction, I repeated, "Have faith... I will wait on you."

"Joseph, let's get something straight. We will never be anything. There is nothing for you to wait on. We are barely even friends, now." She grabbed the door handle again to leave.

Boldness rose up from deep inside me. In a confident voice, I yelled, "Meadow!!! Have faith... I will wait on you."

"You're delusional," she said, with a hopeful grin. The door slammed behind her, and I was left in the shop, alone.

Chapter 10

A Heart of Service

Spring arrived. The same flowers and wild grass arose to greet the town, but a lot had changed. I saw Meadow occasionally. She'd go to school for a few days, and then go missing for a few weeks.

Logan and Big Mike quit coming into the shop. Logan accepted a scholarship to Washington State University, and Big Mike accepted one to the UW. Both were busy training for their first year of college football.

Sarah started dressing like a girl. Who would have thought? Surprisingly, she was turning into quite the looker. She also got more involved in school activities, and became quite the independent woman.

I was getting past Meadow's choices. It hurt me deeply, but I realized that it was out of my control. Mrs. Kat, however, was on my mind daily.

Helping Meadow's mom plagued my conscience. I just wasn't sure how to go about being of assistance to her. I rode by her house on many occasions, but I didn't have the courage to offer my services. Looking back on it, I'm not sure what I was so afraid of. One Sunday afternoon in May, I finally decided to take action.

When I arrived, as usual, Mrs. Kat's house was an atrocious sight. Grass and blackberry bushes ran wild around the entire perimeter of the property. The fence was barely standing, and in desperate need of paint. The porch was cluttered with filth.

I placed my bike against her fence, walked up the creaky porch steps, and knocked on her door. After some delay, Mrs. Kat answered and said, "Hey, I haven't seen you in a while."

I could smell the liquor permeating her breath. Her face was flushed red, and she had a slight slur to her words. It was barely noon, and she was already intoxicated.

"How are you doing, Mrs. Kat?"

"I'm doing fine, honey. But Meadow isn't home."

"That's ok. I'm not here for Meadow. I noticed that your grass is a little tall and I just wanted to offer to mow it," I said, humbly.

"You probably make a good living convincing little, old ladies to empty their pocketbooks while you mow their yards. But I don't believe in paying for something that I can do myself," she said, with extreme sass.

Mrs. Kat was so prideful, and her state of inebriation added to this "virtue." I knew that she couldn't afford to pay for someone to tend her yard, but she would never say that. Instead, she found strength in being rude.

"I'm not going to charge you anything. I just want to help," I said, respectfully.

"Look Joseph, I've been around the block once or twice. I know you're up to something. If you think that doing me a favor or two is going to win over my daughter, then you have another thing coming. It is NOT going to happen."

I strengthened my resolve and argued, "Mrs. Kat, let's get a few things straight. First, you're going to be my mother-in-law someday, so you need to get used to me being around here. Secondly, that has nothing to do with today. Today, I just want to help. I'm going home to grab my push mower, and I will be back."

Angrily she retorted, "Well, it's your time to waste. So I don't care what you do!" She stalked back through her door and slammed it behind her.

I grabbed a push mower, shears, heavy-duty plastic bags, and a few other garden tools that might come in handy. I loaded them up into a wagon that attached to my bike. Then, I made my way back to

Mrs. Kat's house. I didn't even take the time to knock on the door. That yard was a monster and I only had a certain amount of time to tame it. I decided to start on the left side of the house. The corridor between the house and the fence was heavy with tall grass and blackberry bushes. This would be the toughest part of the terrain, so best to tackle it first.

I used shears and the push mower to attack the thorny mess. I tossed the clippings in the large, black, heavy-duty bags. From time to time, my mower would reveal bits of trashy treasure. I collected empty beer cans, numerous whiskey bottles, and old, forgotten toys. I piled these items in front of the house. It took me over an hour to conquer the space.

I cleared a neat path to the back yard. It was a jungle; untouched, and left to its own devices. For a brief moment, I thought about quitting. Then, I thought about Mrs. Kat. She came across as ungrateful. But, on some level, she had to be relieved that the work was being done, and that someone cared about her. No one had done anything for her. And I wasn't going to let her down.

I mowed for hours, disturbing the places the bugs called home. About a quarter of the way through the backyard, I came upon an anthill. I didn't have the tools to take care of something of that magnitude, so I mowed around it. I took the shears and cut the grass against the house and along the fence line. My mower wasn't nimble enough to reach those places. It took me another four hours, but I finished the yard. With a sore lower back and forearms that were on fire, I looked at my handiwork with great satisfaction.

When it was all said and done, I had amassed 11 bags of weeds and grass and 2 bags of garbage. Now it was time to dispose of the waste. I took loads of the brush a few minutes up the road, and I figured I would take the trash to Jimmy. He was a man before his time, the original recycler. He could turn trash into trinkets and sell them to tourists passing through. His souvenir shop was very successful.

I finished my project around dusk and loaded the tools into my wagon. Just as I was about to depart the house, Mrs. Kat stepped out onto her rickety porch.

With tears flowing from her eyes, she said, "Joseph, I'm sorry for how I reacted earlier. The yard looks good. It looks so good."

"The pleasure was all mine, Mrs. Kat."

"Please, won't you come in and have supper with a bitter, old lady? Please, it is the least I can do," she offered, graciously.

Any normal kid would have had to call home and clear it with his parents. But I couldn't remember the last time my parents sat down with me for a Sunday dinner. Still, I didn't want to be rude, and I knew she probably didn't have enough to share. "I don't really want to impose," I said, sincerely. Mrs. Kat grabbed me by the arm and pulled me into her house, insistently.

I had never noticed it before, but Meadow's dad was ripped out of every picture. Mrs. Kat really hated that man. I sat down on her couch. I could feel every, single spring. Mrs. Kat poured herself another stiff drink and served up two bowls of chicken soup. The medley was more broth than chicken or noodles, but the humble meal felt good after a long day of labor. I tried to start a productive conversation during our meal.

"There is an ant hill on the far left side of your backyard. I will come back next week with some spray. Also, your fence really needs repairing in some places. A fresh coat of paint couldn't hurt it, either. I should be able to tackle that next week, too."

Mrs. Kat broke down crying.

"What's the matter, Mrs. Kat? Did I say something wrong?" I asked.

"I haven't seen her in days. She comes and goes as she pleases, and I'm a mess," she said, transparently.

I tried to comfort her by saying, "She is just going through a phase. She'll figure it out. I promise."

"Joseph, she's sneaking into bars already and making all the wrong friends. My girl is gone. And Joseph, I feel so bad for you. You're a really good kid and I know you're doing this to get her attention and it will all be for nothing." Her makeup was running down her face. Her lack of sobriety had not numbed her heart towards her daughter.

"I know that Meadow has been struggling for a while, but I'm sure she'll pull through. Like I said, she isn't the reason I'm here. I did this for you. I got to thinking; you really don't know anyone in town. I just thought I'd help where I could. If you don't mind, I'd like to make this a weekly thing. I will come and help you around the house every Sunday. Is that OK?"

She nodded yes and said, "Joseph, I'm getting really tired. I'm just going to lay here." She laid her head on the end of the couch and was sound asleep in seconds. I covered her with a tattered blanket that sat at the end of the couch. I put the leftover soup in her bare refrigerator and straightened up the small living quarters. The dishes were piled up and the counters looked like they hadn't been wiped down in weeks. After I finished washing both, I gave the linoleum floors a good sweep. I whispered good night to Mrs. Kat and locked the door behind me.

I was exhausted as I rode home, but my heart was full. For some reason, all I could think of was my grandfather. He must have been looking down on me. I imagined him smiling, beaming with a grandfather's pride. I had given everything I had that day.

I watched in wonder as the horizon turned deep purples and pinks. The sun had set, but the residue of God's grace still lingered in the sky. I opened my front door just as the stars showed their bright faces. I walked down the stairs and fell fast asleep.

Chapter 11
Finding My Stride

My junior year snuck up on me, and it was a pleasant surprise. For the first time in my life I felt like I had found my stride. Sarah was voted into student leadership, so I volunteered on a few projects she headed. I also convinced Duke to let the student leadership class conduct their weekly meeting at O'Dell's. This was a welcomed change for some of the students who weren't from our small town. And I enjoyed making new friends.

My slight rise in popularity did not change the core of my routine. I still slaved away at the shop every afternoon. I made good on my promise to Mrs. Kat. I helped her every Sunday. I still served at Papa Pete's ice-cream feeds. And Little PJ and Sarah were still my best friends.

The three of us were really excited for the Winter Solstice. The Winter Solstice was a three-day festival held in Leavenworth, WA. There was nothing else like it in the state. The festival featured a carnival, games, Christmas Tree Lighting, and parade. The parade was the most exciting part for us. Each school around the state entered a float into the parade. The best float won a scholarship for their school, and bragging rights for the year. I was extremely involved in building our school's float. And I couldn't wait to be in the parade. It was the slow season, so I assumed Duke would give me the time off.

Volunteering to build the float required me to wake up at 5:00am, nearly two hours earlier than normal. Given my responsibility to the shop, it was the only time I could work on the project. I biked every morning, in the freezing cold, to Windham. The only person that shared the same level of commitment this early in the morning was Burm.

The theme for our float was Winter Wonderland. It was my job to create the snowdrifts that bordered this massive project. Snowdrifts were tricky at first. While I was engineering these drifts, Burm oversaw other aspects of the float. Needless to say, we got to spend a lot of time together.

Burm had such a great sense of humor. He gave me a hard time no matter how diligently I worked. He'd say, "O'Dell, are you slacking off?" even though he knew I worked harder than most.

He was tough on all of us, but in a good way. We had a competition to win. The plan was to create a wintery paradise. All of the students that volunteered were going to dress up as elves or reindeer. I was elated. I had never had an opportunity to do anything like this before.

I needed to get cleaned up. I only had 10 minutes before the first bell would ring. I walked down the hallway with dried up glue and cotton balls on my hands. Just as I was about to enter the bathroom, I heard someone yell, "Joseph!" It was Sarah.

Her jet-black hair was pulled back and her smile was big. She was a natural beauty and age had done her well. I could still remember when she was just one of the boys. Not now. Sarah traded dirty jeans and a ball cap for an hourglass figure and pouty lips. She scrambled towards me while negotiating an overloaded book bag that slouched on her left shoulder.

Sarah was so driven. I still couldn't believe that she was elected junior class president. She was smart, funny, and had her future all mapped out. Sarah planned to attend Central Washington University and attain a teaching degree. She wanted to teach kindergarten one day. Sarah Dwyer was the complete package. There was no doubt in my mind that she was going to make some guy really happy one day.

"Did you work on the float this morning?" she asked.

"Can't you see the mess all over my hands? You interrupted me before I could wash them," I joked.

"I'm so happy you're helping us. I know that the festival is 6 weeks away, but I'm already working on everyone's costumes. Are you an elf or a reindeer?"

"I think I'm an elf, but put me where you need me."

"That's why I love you, Joseph. I'll see you tonight at the shop. Did you already work out a discount with your dad?"

"Yes, he said we have tons of chocolate ice cream. So there's a deal on anything chocolate. Oh, and he'll cut us a deal on chili-fries, too."

"Perfect. I'll let everyone know. See you later."

I went to the shop after school. It was a Tuesday and, to my surprise, Pastor Paul was there, talking to Duke.

"Duke, we are trying to raise money to start a gift drive for the kids on the south side. We are looking for everyone's help. Most of the establishments in town are putting up a donation jar," Pastor Paul explained. Duke nodded and looked interested. But I knew better. My father's charity was for show.

"I'll do you one better, Paul," Duke boasted. "I will put a jar up, donate 3 percent of my profits from now until the end of the drive, and throw in 10 free ice cream sundaes as a gift."

"You are a Godsend," Pastor Paul said, gratefully. "Hey there, Joseph. How was school?" he asked, directing his attention towards me.

"It was good."

"Duke, you have a fine boy," Pastor Paul declared, before leaving.

Duke's attitude went south. He growled, "Joseph, this shop is in shambles. Things are slow, so you should have no problem waxing the floors, washing the store front, and cleaning out the ice cream bins."

I pleaded, "But sir, the student leadership class is having their weekly meeting here tonight, remember? I talked to you about it last weekend." My rebuttal made Duke furious.

He pounded his fist against the counter and yelled, "Does student leadership pay for anything around here? Do you think I care about your stupid, extracurricular activities? All you guys do is make posters, for God sake! Get your head out of the clouds. This shop should be the most important thing in your life. I'm a man of my word, so I won't cancel your meeting. But, after it's over, you will complete everything on the list. I don't care if you're here until midnight."

"Yes, sir," I meekly replied.

Duke had a knack for losing it like that. I had grown numb to his rants over the years. They didn't even hurt my feelings anymore.

That night, Sarah was in rare form as she led the meeting. She was passionate, funny, and carried herself with confidence and grace. The meeting broke and the students left around 7:00pm. I still had a lot to do. The shop was unusually busy and I hadn't touched Duke's to-do list. I didn't finish until 11:00pm.

That Sunday, I went to Meadow's and helped Mrs. Kat. I shoveled snow and salted her sidewalks, before working inside the house. After shoveling, I took down her dingy wallpaper and prepped the walls for painting. Mrs. Kat poured herself a glass of Jack Daniels and sat on the sofa. She seemed somber.

Mrs. Kat muttered, "I haven't seen her in days, Joseph. I think she's using heroin. She leaves with one set of friends, and a different set drops her off. She's not the same girl she used to be. You should see what she wears. I'm worried sick every day."

"When was the last time you saw her?" I asked, concerned.

"Last Wednesday night. She tried to leave and I got in front of the door. I tried to tell her not to go and that she needed help. I grabbed her arms and saw the track marks. She pushed me out of the way and took off."

I didn't have any magical lines that were going to make her feel better. I didn't have the repair manual to fix their relationship. So I said what was on my heart. "Mrs. Kat, one day your daughter will be back for good."

"You really think so?" she asked, hopefully.

"I know so," I said, with confidence.

"Thank you, Joseph."

"There is no need to thank me, Mrs. Kat. The truth is free." I had to be strong for Mrs. Kat, but I left her house feeling concerned. I addressed the heavens as I walked across the fresh powder. "God, if you're out there, please watch over Meadow. Keep her safe and bring her back to us."

The winter weeks flew by like days. The week of the Winter Solstice Festival came faster than I thought. It was Monday afternoon. I was scheduled to leave for the festival that Thursday, and come back Saturday night. I decided it was time to ask for Duke's permission to go. I figured a few days' notice would be enough.

I knocked on the stockroom door. "Sir, do you mind if I take a couple of days off this week for the Winter Solstice Festival."

"What is the Winter Solstice Festival?" he asked, sternly.

"Well, it's a festival where schools around the state build a float and compete for scholarship money. There is a carnival and a lot of fun stuff to do there. Most of the kids at school are going and..."

"It sounds like a waste of time," Duke interrupted. "I'm going to need you to work at the shop."

"But sir, I've worked really hard on the float and..."

"I said no. That is the end of it," he snapped. I was crushed. Why was he so hateful? What did I do to him? What did the world do to Duke O'Dell and why did I have to receive the brunt of it.

I went to bed that night, teary-eyed and disappointed. How was I going to tell Burm and the rest of the leadership class that I couldn't participate?

I rode my bike to school early the next morning. I discovered Burm adding the finishing touches to the float. I approached him with my head held low and my shoulders slumped over. "Burm, do you mind if we talk?" I asked, sadly.

Sensing my demeanor, he spared me the jokes and said, "Of course, what's going on O'Dell?"

"I can't go to the Winter Solstice Festival."

"Why not? You were so excited about it. Is there anything I can do to help?"

"You can't help me. I really don't want to get into it. Just know that I want to be there, but I can't. I appreciate everything, Burm." I shook his hand and made my way to the door.

"Joseph."

"Yes?"

"You have a good heart, kid. Don't lose it."

Only seven customers walked through the doors of O'Dell's between Thursday and Saturday. I was so mad at Duke. He didn't need me. He was motivated by pure bitterness when he forbade me to go to the festival.

That Saturday night, I went home and sat at my grandfather's writing desk. I stared at its top for what seemed like hours.

———— ❧ ————

"He was so hard on you, Mr. Joseph."

"Yes he was. I didn't know why he was so angry, at the time. But later, I would discover the source of his pain. And, believe it or not, I was the one being hard on him."

"What do you mean?" Bridgett Marie asked, confused.

"People don't start off bitter. Traumatic events molded Duke into the man I grew up with. It will make sense shortly."

"Mr. Joseph, you don't look so good. Can I get you something... some water maybe?"

"I'll be fine."

———— ❧ ————

Chapter 12

Overdose

Junior year passed like a summer's breeze. I learned a lot, and not just from my classes. I had inadvertently become a student of people.

Some days it was tough to look at those around me. It felt like the majority of them weren't happy with their lives or themselves. They walked around pretending – lost souls trying to find their own way. In most cases, the blind were leading the blind. And I was a member of their fraternity. Observing them was like staring in the mirror. We were scared and humbled by the weight of our own insignificance. We were looking for something to fill the loneliness. But today would be one of those days when I would crash into a whole lot of humanity, and I'd be anything but lonely.

It was the middle of summer and the shop was busier than usual. It was as if the tourists and locals declared a national ice cream day, and O'Dell's was the place to join in the festivities. I worked non-stop alongside Duke to provide some good, old-fashioned service with a smile.

The day was coming to an end when I received the most unexpected visitor. Mrs. Kat burst through the doors of the shop. "Joseph, you have to help me. She almost killed herself!" she yelled.

"Mrs. Kat, slow down. What's going on?"

"I can't do this by myself!" she shrieked. "You have to go with me!" The remaining customers were quiet as church mice. Mrs. Kat's erratic behavior had put every, last person into a state of shock. Duke's face wore a thick coat of embarrassment.

"Joseph," said Duke, "why don't you go and help this lovely lady with whatever she needs... now!" Translation: *"Get out and quit embarrassing me and, rest assured, we will have a long, brutal conversation, later."* Duke was struggling to keep a calm demeanor. All eyes were on us. The hushed whispers were already beginning to circulate, and it didn't take long for news to travel in towns like ours.

Mrs. Kat and I rushed out of the shop and hopped into her rusty, '58 ford. I had seen the bucket (which she referred to as Old Betsy) parked outside of her house, but I had never seen it move. I sat on the weathered, leather seat, as we rode to the hospital. Mrs. Kat kept muttering things that were barely understandable.

She would begin a sentence with, "How could she do this..." but, as her sentences dragged on, they transformed into nothing more than mumbling.

I should have been driving. I could smell the whiskey on Mrs. Kat's breath. It was even permeating through her skin. The entire vehicle smelled like "last call" at the local pub.

When we arrived at the hospital, Mrs. Kat almost tackled the first nurse she saw. "Where is my daughter? Where is my DAUGHTER? You called me and said she was here! So, where is she?" Mrs. Kat badgered.

"Ma'am you need to calm down," the nurse sternly said.

"My daughter almost killed herself hanging around with her good-for-nothing friends! How do you expect me to calm down? WHERE IS SHE?"

Another nurse approached us and asked, "Are you Meadow's mom?"

"Yes! Is she OK?"

"She is doing better, ma'am. Follow me." The nurse led us down a maze of long, sterile hallways, until we arrived at room 134. The nurse stood in front of the door and wouldn't let us enter, at first. Her nametag read: Peggy.

"The last few hours have been very tough for Meadow," explained Nurse Peggy, sounding very concerned. "She is just starting to come around. Ma'am, I know this is probably really hard on you. But I'm going to need you to be supportive. The last thing your daughter needs right now is added stress on her body."

Peggy opened the door and allowed us to enter. Meadow was hooked to an I.V. and barely awake. It was tough seeing her in that bed. It almost made me cry. But I knew that I had to be strong for Mrs. Kat. I noticed cuts across Meadow's arms. She also had a deep gash just above her left eyebrow. It was freshly stitched.

"Where did she get those cuts?" I asked the nurse.

"Whoever she was with didn't much care about her," said Peggy. "They threw her from a moving car, right outside the hospital. I'm sure they didn't want to be connected with her overdose. One of the nurses saw the whole thing." Her words were matter-of-fact, but there was compassion in her face when she said, "She gave us quite a scare last night. We thought we were going to lose her, but we didn't. This young lady is a fighter."

Ignoring the nurse's instructions, Mrs. Kat lost it. She ran over to Meadow's bedside and grabbed her by the collar. "How could you do this to yourself? Hey you selfish... wake up! You could have died, you little tramp!"

"Get off me!" Meadow weakly responded.

"You could have died! You could have died!" Mrs. Kat yelled, repeatedly. Nurse Peggy tried her best to get in-between them.

Feebly, Meadow glared at her mother. Her voice was faint, but her anger was not. "Get off me. I hate you so much. I wish I would have died, then I wouldn't have to deal with you," she said, to Mrs. Kat.

Nurse Peggy, losing her patience, demanded, "Ma'am, you need to leave this room, NOW, before I call security."

I grabbed Mrs. Kat and held her as tight as I could. I could feel the tension in my arms. "Let it go. She's OK, Mrs. Kat. Everything is going to be OK... Just let it go," I said, repeatedly. She relaxed some. Then, she sobbed in the nook between my neck and shoulder. I held her for a few moments, and reassured her. Then, I said, "Mrs. Kat, please go with Nurse Peggy and get some coffee. I will stay here with Meadow."

"OK, Joseph," she muttered.

Meadow's voice was hoarse, but full of contempt. Lashing out, she rasped, "She is such an actress. I bet the old drama queen has you fooled into thinking that she actually cares."

"Meadow, what happened?" I asked.

"It's none of your damn business. And I'm not a junkie, so I don't need you feeling sorry for me. And I don't need you judging me, either. In fact, I don't need you at all!"

"I'm not judging you. And I don't think you're a junkie. I just want to know what happened."

"I was just having some fun, and it got a little out of hand, that's all. It doesn't matter. Like I said, it's none of your business," she sneered.

Her words angered me. I had never lost my patience with Meadow. But, there's a first time for everything. I raised my voice. "Don't you ever say something like that to me again! I mean it, Meadow! You are my concern, every day. I wake up every day, thinking about you. I pray every night. And all I ask for is your safety. I stick up for you. People laugh at me and call me stupid, but I don't care. And did you know that every Sunday I go to your mother's house? I keep her company while you're gone. I can't fix everything, but I do what I can. So you need to know that your life has been, and will always be, my business." I stormed toward the door.

Meadow called out, "JoJo, please don't leave." I sat down heavily in the chair next to her bed. She reached for my hand and said, "JoJo, have you ever wanted to be someone you're not? Or put on a mask in hopes that the new you will hide the pain?"

"Yes," I said, certainly.

"The new friends, the drugs, the alcohol, the sex... they help me cope with my biggest fear."

"What is your biggest fear?" I asked, sincerely.

"Discovering who I really am. That's the difference between you and me. You have the courage to be yourself. And that is why you're my hero, JoJo. You're my hero."

I kissed her hand and held back my tears. Meadow was still a little out of it. She gave me a weak smile and closed her eyes.

"Joseph, I'm getting tired. Do you mind doing me a favor before you go?"

"Anything," I said.

"Can you sing me a song?"

"I'm not much of a singer."

"It doesn't matter. I just want you to sing me a song. Please?"
I sang the only song I could think of.

He's got the whole world in His hands
He's got the whole world in His hands
He's got the whole world in His hands
He's got the whole world in His hands

He's got you and me Meadow, in His hands
He's got you and me Meadow, in His hands
He's got you and me Meadow, in His hands
He's got the whole world in His hands

Meadow fell fast asleep. The only noises in the room were the beeping of the monitors and the sound of her breathing. She hadn't had this type of peace in a long time. I didn't want to leave her side, but I really needed to get back to the shop. Duke was going to kill me. I decided I would leave her a note. I grabbed a pen and a loose piece of blank paper from a pad on the nightstand next to her.

I started what I thought would be a simple note, but it became more than that. As I finished writing, I scrawled *Battered Angel* across the top. Before leaving the room, I leaned over and whispered softly, "Have faith... I will wait on you."

Mrs. Kat was sitting in the waiting room. Her hands were shaking uncontrollably. She could barely keep her coffee stable as her hands grasped the white, Styrofoam cup. I sat down next to her on one of the stiff, waiting room chairs.

"Joseph, I just don't know what I'm going to do with her. She's trying to do this to me on purpose, isn't she? She blames me for her dad... for everything. Yeah, I might drink, but I'm dealing with a lot."

"Mrs. Kat," I said, softly, "I don't believe that Meadow is trying to hurt you. Both of you are hurt. You're both trying to cope. But, in coping in your individual ways, you're not only hurting yourselves, you're destroying each other in the process."

Mrs. Kat didn't care for my insight. I had inadvertently touched a nerve. Coldly, she said, "Who asked you? What do you know? You're just a dumb kid, like her. You don't know anything."

"You're right, Mrs. Kat. I'm just a kid. I'll make my own way back to the shop. I love you both." I handed her the poem and added, "Please give this to Meadow when she wakes up."

As I left, Mrs. Kat unfolded the paper and read:

Battered Angel

You've fallen from nowhere
To a world that beats you black and blue
I try to no avail
My arms aren't strong enough to catch you

I'd take your place if I could
Patched wounds and I.V. occupied veins
Stitched cuts and sticky sutures
From a stiff chair, I watch as you lay

Pain muffled by pills
Girl in the sterile room
Winter brings about the harshest chill
Before the flowers bloom

So, escape to the sweetest dreams
I pray you will do the same
White garment and beautiful wings
Walk in the paradise from whence you came

Worry no more
Find peace in this truth
Soar on the skies of your mind
Battered Angel, it's my turn to guard you

By the time I got back to O'Dell's, Duke was just closing up. My heart beat rapidly and my stomach rolled like an angry sea. I was in for it.

Duke gave me an icy stare. He barked, "I'm going to make this short and sweet. You are allowed to be dumb, *once*, as a teenager. *That* was your one chance at being dumb. I will not be embarrassed like that ever again. I don't want to hear anything about you hanging around this girl or her crazy mom again. They are riffraff."

"But Sir..."

"Don't 'but sir' me. This conversation is over. Now get out of my face and get these tables wiped down and this damn floor swept."

I took my time closing the shop. I cleaned for three hours. I got home around 9:30pm. I was about to retire for the night, but the sliding glass door off the living room was open. My mother was in the backyard, watering her plants.

So many feelings bubbled up inside of me. I felt like I needed a mom more than ever. I walked out into the backyard and muttered, "Mom?"

"Yes, Joseph?" Her back was turned to me and her voice was lifeless and monotone.

"I really need to talk to you."

"About what?" she sighed, as if I was interrupting her personal time.

"Well... umm... I... umm... I... was... was... just wondering... umm..."

"Just get to the point," she interrupted. "I'm busy."

"Do you regret having me? Was I some sort of mistake?" I asked.

My mother's back was still turned, but her posture stiffened, and I could tell that I had her attention. Instead of watering her plants back and forth, she held the hose in one place, drowning the unfortunate plants beneath the spray. I waited for her response, but the awkward silence did not come to an end. Eventually, I took her inability to answer the question as a definite yes. I left her alone and went to my room.

Shortly after, I heard a tapping on the small glass that let light into my basement room. It was Little PJ. I went upstairs and let him in.

"Hey, stranger. I came by earlier, but you weren't here. Where were you?" he asked.

I told Little PJ every, crazy detail of what had happened that night. I expected him to tell some jokes, or make fun of the situation, but his next words were unexpected.

"Joseph, do you think you're doing the right things for the wrong reasons?" Little PJ asked.

Sensing he had more to say, I snapped, "I'm fed up with everyone, so stop beating around the bush and tell me what's on your mind."

"Do you want me to be honest?" he asked, irritated.

"Just say what you have to say," I escalated.

"I think you're wasting your time. I think Meadow and her mom take advantage of you. And I think you let them, because you think Meadow is going to like you one day. That's stupid, Joseph. Girls like Meadow don't notice guys like you or me. But they will use us. I know you think she's going to change, but people don't change."

"Not you, too!" I scolded. "What is going on around here? I expect this from Duke, or from the gossipers in town... but not from you. You're supposed to be my friend."

"Joseph, you're more than a best friend to me. You're family. You're even closer to me than my real family. With them, I feel like I get in the way. I'm just another mouth to feed. I go to school and don't work the fields. It's almost like they hold it against me. But I feel important when I'm around you. I feel like somebody."

"Little PJ, remember when we were first assigned to be locker partners in seventh grade?"

"Yeah. How could I forget?"

"Remember how you didn't talk to me for weeks? I invited you to the shop and you wouldn't come. I tried to be your friend but you wouldn't let me. Do you remember?"

"If people weren't talking about my size, they were pointing out my freckles. I thought you were going to be like everyone else."

"But, was I like everyone else?"

"No. You turned out to be different. It was my birthday and none of my family remembered. Mrs. Pittman made the announcement in class, but no one wanted to sing *Happy Birthday*. You brought me an ice-cream sundae after you got off work. No one had ever done anything like that for me..."

"And we've been friends ever since," I interrupted.

"Yes, we have," Little PJ agreed.

"So, tell me, what changed? What made you hang with me after your birthday?"

"Because I knew you were different," he explained.

"And because you trusted me, Little PJ. You already said people don't change. Well, you trusted me before. So... trust me now."

"OK. But I have one, last question."

"What?" I asked.

"What do I have to do to get something to eat around here?" he joked.

We laughed together for the rest of the night.

Chapter 13

The Prom

It was the end of my senior year. Everyone's life plans were working out great. I was honored, even humbled, to see how my friends had grown. We were still a raggedy bunch, but somehow we were making the best of everything life had thrown at us.

Sarah had become the most popular girl at school. She was ambitious, gorgeous, and an absolute joy to be around. How she preserved her "girl next door" attitude was beyond me. She was accepted into Central Washington University early that year. Her dreams of being an elementary school teacher were right around the corner.

Little PJ didn't change one bit. He never missed an opportunity to make light of a situation. His antics landed him in the principal's office from time to time, but he never got into any real trouble. Despite his playful demeanor, Little PJ was very driven. His plan was to get as far from this town as possible and make it big. He was well on his way to both. He was accepted to Seattle University, where he planned to obtain his law degree.

I had been accepted to the University of Washington. I loved writing and I had a heart for people. I decided to pursue a career in journalism. I believed, one day, my stories would be a catalyst for change. I wanted to write about the people and places humanity forgot about.

Duke said my aspirations were a waste of time. He made it very clear that if I planned to go into journalism, he would not support me financially. This did not detour me. I was confident that I could make my own way. I had experience running O'Dell's, and there were plenty of restaurants in the Seattle area. I was sure that one of them would find me employable. I didn't care if I had to secure two or more jobs; I would pay my way through school. I didn't plan to cut Duke and O'Dell's off cold turkey. I would come home during the summers and work in the shop during the busy season. That is, unless Duke found a suitable replacement for me.

Little PJ, Sarah, and I decided to go to the Senior Prom together. It was Sarah's idea. She could have gone with any guy she wanted. She was asked at least twice a day. But Sarah was the type of girl that didn't want to complicate things.

She said, "I want to end senior year with my two favorite guys in the entire world."

Going to the prom together was a win-win for all of us. Sarah didn't want some guy professing his love to her all night, Little PJ couldn't find a date, and I was too busy waiting on "you know who." I had a feeling that this would be a night to remember. Unfortunately, it would be just that, but for all the wrong reasons.

I gave myself the once-over in a mirror that leaned against a wall in my bedroom. I wasn't on a 'real' date, so a tux would be a little too much. So, I put on my best suit.

I could hear Duke's heavy feet making their way down the stairs. I was shocked. Duke rarely visited my room. There was something different about him. He was wearing a smile for some reason.

"Son, I heard you're going to the prom with Sarah. She has grown to be a real looker. Pastor Paul was in earlier this week and he told me you two were going to the prom together. I can't believe it. My son is going to the prom with the prettiest girl in school, and the pastor's daughter, at that. So, what are your plans tonight?"

I couldn't believe that Duke and I were going to have an actual conversation. It felt nice. I explained, "Well, Sarah, Little PJ and I were planning to..."

"What do you mean, Little PJ?" he asked, in an irritated tone.

"It was Sarah's idea to..."

"Do you have to do everything with Little PJ?" Duke interrupted. "Is he your girlfriend or something? Jesus!!! Why would you mess it up with a girl like Sarah? She isn't a total waste of your time like that floozy you were chasing."

"Don't talk about Meadow like that!" I said, sternly.

Duke was caught off-guard by my outburst. He walked a few steps closer to me and poked me in the chest. "I know what this is about," he said, obnoxiously. "You and Sarah can't go alone, because your make-believe girlfriend might find out. Isn't it? Isn't it?"

I kept quiet. I didn't want to provoke him any further. But my silence pushed him over the edge. "Get over it, Joseph!" Duke yelled. "What are you, in love with her or something? Why are you wasting your time? Have I taught you nothing? She's a junkie and a whore for God's sake!"

Without considering the consequences, I shouted, "Who are you to judge anyone... Or talk about love, for that matter? You're just perfect, aren't you? You have it all figured out, don't you? You and mom sit around here like roommates. She's depressed and you're too self-absorbed and busy with the shop to care. I've never seen you two kiss or hug. We barely ever sit down to dinner. You guys don't even celebrate my birthday. Is that normal? No it isn't! All you care about is what people think. That's the only reason you're even concerned with me impressing Sarah. It's because me dating the Pastor's daughter makes you look good. You don't know anything about what it means to love someone. You could care less about your family. At least Meadow doesn't pretend to be someone she isn't. And that is more than I can say for you. So who are you to judge, Duke?"

A split second later, I felt the inside of Duke's coarse hand against the left side of my face. His paw connected cleanly and my ear rang like a cymbal. The force of the blow threw off my equilibrium and sent me stumbling backwards. Duke did not stop his attack. He charged in my direction, grabbed me by the collar, lifted me off of my feet, and rammed me into the wall. I felt the paint and drywall collapse under the pressure. He brought my face within an inch of his.

"You don't know anything about family, real love, or real loss!" Duke lashed out. "And you don't know me half as well as you think you do!" He punched the wall, just to the right of my face, repeatedly. The forceful blows went clear through the stud. His knuckles bled. The muscles on his forearms flexed as he clutched my collar tighter.

Then, surprisingly, his bottom lip started quivering and his eyes welled with tears. He drew his bloody right fist back, and held me against the wall with his left. He wanted to knock me out. But he didn't. He looked at me for a few, uncomfortable seconds. Shivering, he let me go. Duke walked towards the steps. I should have kept my mouth shut, but part of me wanted him to finish me. I didn't care anymore.

"I know more than you think," I ranted. "I know that you make me feel small because, on some level, you're small and weak. And I know that I've grown to hate you. I HATE YOU!"

Duke clenched the knob of the staircase banister with his massive hand. His swollen veins pumped blood through his arms. I braced myself for Duke to turn and charge me again. I held my breath for what seemed like an eternity. But he never came after me. He just dragged his heavy feet up the steps.

Telling my father that I hated him was an action that I would regret for the rest of my life. For the first time, I had sunk to Duke's level. Why didn't I just ignore his taunts? Why couldn't I just conduct business as usual? I should have shown Duke the same grace that I had shown everyone else. I didn't mean what I said. I didn't hate him. But some words can't be taken back, no matter how sorry you are.

"Mr. Joseph, let me get you a tissue."

"Thank you, honey. Learn from my example. Never use the word 'hate'," I said, through tears.

"Mr. Joseph, you don't have to finish. I can go back to cleaning."

"There is no doubt that this was a stormy time in my life. Believe it or not, it was just the tip of the iceberg. You won't believe what happened next. But I just have to tell you... I know you don't understand right now. But it is so very important for me to finish this story. Please stay and listen," I pleaded.

"Yes, of course I will stay and listen." By this time, Bridgett Marie was grabbing the Kleenex, too. "OK, Mr. Joseph. I'm not going anywhere."

My shirt collar was wrinkled where Duke had grabbed me. I didn't have time to iron it. I decided not to focus on it. I went up the stairs and grabbed some scissors off the kitchen counter. Then, I went into my mother's garden and cut one of her roses. I knew that she would notice. Maybe it would be a good thing. Maybe it would motivate her to talk to me. I really didn't care at this point. I just wanted to be with my friends.

The plan was for Sarah to pick up me and Little PJ in her dad's truck. I left the house and paced up and down the block. I was restless. I just needed to go. Finally, Sarah showed up.

In a flirtatious tone, she said, "Hey handsome... do you need a lift?" I found myself smiling. I hopped into the truck and the world was OK again. My episode with Duke became a faint memory.

I couldn't help but notice how beautiful Sarah was. Her dress was aqua blue, and the color made her eyes sparkle. Her hair was pulled up into a neat bun with wispy tendrils hanging on either side of her face. The dress was fitted and accentuated curves that she usually kept hidden. She looked fantastic.

In an earnest voice she asked, "Do I look OK?"

I couldn't believe the question. How could a girl like her, so gorgeous, so confident, have a moment of such insecurity? At that moment, I realized that we, as people, are more alike than we are different. Even the brightest corner of humanity can feel dim at times.

"Sarah, you look great," I said, sincerely. She smiled, leaned in, and gave me a kiss on the cheek. I gave her the rose that I'd pilfered from Gloria's garden. Then we set off to pick up Little PJ.

We drove by Meadow's house on our way. I couldn't help but look. I hadn't seen her in a couple months. Secretly, I hoped that she might be on her porch. Maybe she would decide to go to the dance with us.

It would be like junior high all over again. In my heart, I knew that it was just wishful thinking. We drove through Rosy Glenn Trailer Park and pulled up to Little PJ's home.

I knocked a few times, but Little PJ didn't answer. His brother finally came to the door and explained that Little PJ had food poisoning. I could hear him throwing up from the door. I peeked my head around his brother and called out to him, "I'll catch up with you later, buddy."

"Where is Little PJ?" Sarah questioned.

"He got food poisoning," I giggled.

"Are you serious? He's going to miss the prom. I guess it's just me and you, Joseph."

"Yes, I guess it's just us," I agreed.

"That's not a bad thing... right?" she asked.

"No, it's not bad at all," I assured her.

"There will be some guys that are really upset with me," she noted. "I told everyone that asked me to the prom that I was going with my two best friends. Now, it looks like I'm on a date."

"That's not a bad problem to have," I laughed.

We danced all night. And, for the second time, I was the envy of all the guys in the room. In junior high, I danced with Meadow while all the guys watched, and now it was happening with Sarah. I tried not to see it as an official date. But it was tough not to. I was having too good of a time. Even so, I looked up from time to time, scanning the dance floor for Meadow. If she came, she would bring an older guy with movie star looks. That was just her style. I would be envious, but I would gladly trade that discomfort for the opportunity to see her. I wanted to know that she was alright.

"Are you having a good time?" Sarah asked, breaking my thoughts.

"Do you even have to ask? I'm having a great time."

"Do you wish Little PJ was here?"

Focusing my attention fully on her, I said, "I wouldn't change anything, Sarah."

It occurred to me that something more than friendship was stirring up between us. It was an energy that came from some place deep inside. I had to push it down. I had to deny it. I was saving myself for someone else. It probably sounds stupid today. But, at the time, I was totally convinced that what I was feeling for Sarah was wrong. Could it be love? Was it heightened infatuation? Whatever it was, it felt great.

Sarah and I left the dance holding hands. Her head rested against my shoulder as we made our way back to the pickup. She smelled so good. She asked, "Joseph, do you have to go home right away?"

My palms were sweaty. Her question made me nervous. The moment made me nervous. I thought to myself, "Don't get ahead of yourself. She probably wants to hang out as friends."

"Home is the last place I want to be," I admitted.

"Is everything OK?" she asked.

I thought of the words I'd said to Duke. The tongue is such a hypocrite. It has the ability to restore broken dreams, build people up, and speak life into a dreadful situation. But the same tongue can tear others down, and conjure up total chaos. Earlier that evening, I'd let my tongue do the latter. I didn't want to bring down the mood of the night. This was an important night for Sarah, and I didn't want to ruin it. I decided that fibbing would be the best approach.

"Everything is fine. What do you want to do?"

"I want to take you to the most beautiful place in town," she said.

It didn't take me long to realize where we were going. When we pulled up to the sign that read, "Private Property No Trespassing," I chuckled to myself. It was my family's property. Sarah had no idea that I had been to this place hundreds of times.

"We have to be really careful, Joseph," she whispered.

"I know. This is private property," I laughed.

"What is so funny?" she asked.

"Oh, nothing," I said, stifling my laughter.

We scaled up the incline at the start of the trail. It was a lot more difficult to do it at night, wearing fancy clothes. I took the lead and helped Sarah through the rougher parts of the terrain. She instructed me on how to conquer the hill, as if I was a visitor to this place. I didn't want to spoil it for her so I kept up the ruse.

We got to the summit and the view was breathtaking. The stars looked close enough to grab, and the moon was full. There wasn't a cloud in the sky.

Sarah said, "Isn't the view fantastic? Wasn't it worth the climb?"

"Yes."

We walked a few yards before finding a grassy patch to sit on. I laid my jacket on the damp earth so that she wouldn't get her dress dirty. I tried my best to make light of a very romantic setting.

"Sarah, how did you do it?"

"How did I do what?"

"How did you manage to get the attention of every guy at the dance? You should have seen them. They were all drooling over you. There was a lot of angry girls at that dance, trust me," I laughed.

Sarah flirtatiously shoved me on the shoulder and said, "They weren't all staring at me. Besides, *all* the guys don't matter. All that matters is that I had fun with you."

Before I knew it, Sarah was sliding her hand over mine. My stomach was filled with butterflies and I could feel my palms beginning to sweat. I didn't realize that I was looking in the opposite direction until she said my name.

"Joseph?"

"Yes?"

She took her time. She cleared her throat. Whatever she was going to say had to be pretty heavy. I could just feel it. She muttered, "Joseph, what if I told you that I see you?"

I didn't really understand where she was going with this conversation. But I sensed a certain level of vulnerability. Sarah was about to share something with me that she had held very close. I could tell. I had been in her position with Meadow a time or two.

"I'm not sure that I know what you mean," I said, honestly.

"In order to see someone," she explained, "really see someone, you have to be able to look past the distractions. I see past the work you do at the shop for a father who doesn't appreciate you. I see past the way you go above and beyond for Meadow and her mom. I even see past the constant friend you've been to me and Little PJ, and how you give to everyone around you. People might look at you and say, 'Here is a guy who likes to do for others. Here is the definition of a nice guy.' But, Joseph, you're more than just a nice guy who does nice things. I see past your actions and I see your heart. Your heart is the most beautiful thing in the world to me. You are the most amazing, wonderful, decent person I've ever met. I am truly blessed to be your friend. And, if I had to be totally honest, well... I would like to be much more. Everything happens for a reason. Little PJ being sick wasn't an accident. And I know that you felt something tonight, too."

"Sarah, where is this all coming from?" I asked, nervously. Sarah gazed at the stars for a few moments before answering. She composed herself and slowly spoke.

"I've had a crush on you for as long as I can remember, since junior high, at least. And, just when I was building up the courage to tell you how I felt, Meadow came into the picture. Joseph, in a couple of months we will all be going our separate ways. But I knew if I didn't tell you how I felt, I would always regret it. I love you, Joseph. I always have."

Tears ran down her face as she finished. It took me a while to respond. Sarah squirmed where she sat. My silence made her uncomfortable. She was waiting for me to say something – anything, for that matter. I'd had no idea that she felt this way about me. I searched for the right words. I didn't want to say anything wrong, but I desperately needed to break the silence.

"Sarah, I don't know what to say. I mean, I think you're great but..." I began, lamely. Sarah cut me off before I could finish. She got up and darted for the hill. "Sarah, wait," I called after her.

She shouted, "Forget I said anything."

Sarah bounded down the hill like a mountain goat. I had a tough time keeping up. I was concerned for her safety. I called out to her on a number of occasions but she didn't respond. I could see her approaching the bottom of the hill, so I broke into an all-out sprint. I knew that it was dangerous, but I needed to catch up with her. Out of breath, I reached the truck. I was exhausted. I placed my hands on the hood to support my weight.

"Sarah, wait," I gasped.

"Joseph, I've waited long enough. You don't have to explain. I get it. I'm not pretty enough..."

"No, that isn't it," I interrupted.

"So, then, I'm not smart enough... or is it because I'm too independent?"

"It's not that either. I think it's great that you're so independent."

"Maybe it's because I don't sleep around, and you think I won't be exciting enough for you."

"How could you even say that?"

"Then what is it, Joseph? WHAT IS IT? What is wrong with me?" she yelled, hysterically. Her face, drowned in tears. My heart hurt for her. I knew exactly how she felt.

I explained, "It would be unfair. You are a beautiful person, Sarah. But I have feelings... very strong feelings for someone and..."

She interrupted, "Joseph, why are you waiting on her? What makes Meadow so special?"

I hadn't told anyone why I was waiting on Meadow. It was my most guarded secret. Besides, if I shared it with Sarah, she'd think I was crazy. I stood there, unable to speak. Sarah decided to break the silence herself.

"Just get in the car."

"But Sarah... let me explain," I contested.

"Fine, if you don't want to get in, I'll leave."

Sarah put the pickup in reverse and left me on the side of the road.

I woke up early the next morning with a very heavy heart. I had somehow managed to hurt two people in one night. I decided to write a letter of apology to Duke. I sat at the kitchen table with paper and pen in hand.

Duke had beaten me to the punch. On the table lay an envelope with my name written across it. It was my father's handwriting. Inside was a wad of money, a note, and a bus ticket to Seattle for 8:00pm that very night. I unfolded the note and read the terse words.

Joseph,
Your employment at O'Dell's is officially terminated. You will find a bus ticket and enough funds for incidentals.

It was clear. The damage was irreversible. Duke was kicking me out. I only had a few hours to say my goodbyes. I knew that I would be OK. I had to execute my original plan a few weeks early. I called Windham High a few days later. With so little left of the school year, and my college acceptance already in place, it was surprisingly easy to work out the details. They would send my diploma by mail, but I would miss the graduation celebration.

I packed a couple of backpacks. When it came down to it, I didn't need much. I would make up for anything I had to leave behind, in Seattle. I took a shower, collected my bags, and put them next to the door. It was time to say my goodbyes.

I started with my mother. If Duke wanted to say goodbye to me, he would have given me the envelope in person. I walked out to the garden where Gloria was tending to her roses.

"Mom, I'm leaving."

"I figured you'd be leaving, sooner or later."

"Well, I'll be back next summer," I said, hopefully.

She didn't respond to me. I tried hugging her. She did not hug me back. Her body was stiff and cold.

I kneeled next to her and said, "Mom, I'm not sure why we never had a real relationship. But I want you to know that I've always needed you. I've never held your silence against you. I have no ill will or bitterness towards you. And I'll be more than willing to accept your love when you're ready to give it."

I decided to leave her to her garden. A single tear cascaded down her cheek. I kissed her on the forehead and left the house I was raised in.

I went to Jimmy's Souvenir Shop. His store was closed on Sunday, but it was an emergency. I had to get something for Meadow before I left. He lived above the shop. If I yelled and knocked long enough, he'd answer.

Jimmy's VW Bug was parked outside. There was a good chance he was home. I banged on the storefront until he answered.

"What can I do you for, Joseph?" Jimmy asked, with a smile. Jimmy Heffernan was in his mid-fifties. His silver hair was just starting to recede. Jimmy had an average build, a baby face, and sparkly blue eyes.

"I have to head off to school earlier than I expected. I really need your help," I explained, sadly.

"You know I'll help you with whatever I can. Come on in," he said.

Jimmy was a tinkerer. The walls of his shop were lined with local photos, contraptions, and junk that he marketed as 'northwest' art. It was a quaint but crowded space.

I looked at the displays and said, "I need a special gift for a special person."

"So, you need to get Meadow something before you go, huh?" he interjected.

"How did you know?" I asked, surprised.

"Now Joseph, you know this town ain't big enough for secrets," he said, with a grin.

"Isn't that the truth," I agreed.

"I have exactly what you need. Give me one sec," he said, before scurrying to the back.

Jimmy brought back a wood box. He sat the simple box on the counter. It was big enough to carry a pair of shoes. He gazed at the box as if it held the meaning of life itself. He pointed at the front door and said, "The most beautiful woman I had ever seen walked through those very doors. It happened years ago. I don't even think you were born. She wore a long, white dress with the most extraordinary red belt. I even commented on the fancy thing. They didn't make clothes like that around here. I asked her, 'How can I help you ma'am?' 'I'm looking for inspiration,' she said. She hummed an infectious tune while she browsed the shop. She walked around humming that tune, until she came across one of your grandfather's paintings. She pulled it off the wall and asked, 'How much?' I answered, 'The painting isn't for sale...'"

I interrupted Jimmy's story and asked, "What did my grandfather paint for you?" Jimmy canvassed the shop before answering. There was magic in his eyes.

"It was a picture of me," he continued, "behind this very counter. He painted it on opening day. Joe believed that going into business for yourself was special. He said, maintaining the 'opening day' excitement, every day, is the key to success. The painting was a reminder to do just that."

"Did you give it to her?" I asked, curiously.

"Joseph, the pretty little gal wouldn't take no for an answer. After tons of back and forth, she finally said, 'I'll tell you what, Jimmy... I will make you an offer you can't refuse. You said the painting is priceless, and I can respect that. I have something priceless, too. You were admiring my belt earlier. You have good taste Jimmy. I had it custom made. This is the only one of its kind in the world. So, how about a trade, something priceless for something priceless?' Joseph, something special happens when you give so much to someone you know so little. We spent an hour making small talk. Before she left, I asked, 'Is there a chance I'll see you again?' She said, 'I live in New York. I'm just passing through. But, if you're ever in my neck of the woods, look me up. Maybe I'll let you take me out to dinner.' 'But wait,' I said. 'I don't even know your name.' 'Oh, you'll figure it out,' she said, with a devilish grin. I asked, 'What are you doing so far away from home?' 'Like I said before, I'm looking for inspiration,' she said, gave me a wink, and left the shop. A few months later, I hear that tune she hummed on the radio. Then, a lady sang about this very shop. It was her, Joseph!"

"She wasn't lying to you, Jimmy. She had the music but she needed the words. You inspired her!" I said, excited.

"Damn right I did," he said, proudly.

"I took her belt and turned it into two bracelets. I planned to find her in New York, give her one, and keep the other. This way, we'd always be connected. I was packing my car. A couple of buddies saw me and walked over. I told them about the adventure I was about to go on. It was the worst mistake of my life. They made me feel lower than dirt, Joseph. They reminded me of how regular I was. By the time they were done, I'd unpacked for good. I had convinced myself there was nothing for me outside this dingy town. She got married a few years later. And that was that."

Jimmy opened the box. There were the two bracelets. They were the most beautiful things I had ever seen. He shoved the box in my direction and said, "Take them."

"I couldn't," I retorted.

"Yes, you can. I have no use for them now."

I dug through my pockets and asked, "How much do I owe you?"

"You don't owe me anything. I wouldn't have them if it weren't for your grandfather's painting. You have Joe's spirit."

Head bowed, I muttered, "I don't know about that, Jimmy."

"Joseph, take it from an old fool. You, I, everyone, we were all put on this earth to do one thing. That one thing is to love. To love without reservation is the greatest thing someone can do. It's the way you love Meadow. You support her in spite of what she does, and what others say. There is something honorable about that... something simple and pure. All those people judging you are cowards. They had the same opportunity to love in the same way, but they chose not to. And now, they want to spread their hopelessness and regret. Don't you dare listen to them, Joseph."

"I understand, Jimmy," I said, with a new sense of worth.

Jimmy pulled the bracelets out of the box and sat them on the counter. The red leather straps and metal clasp made for the perfect contrast. He grabbed a nail, heated the tip of it on a stove, and said, "Now, let's make these bracelets yours. Would you like me to carve her name in one and your name in the other?"

"I have an even better idea," I said, delighted. "On one of the bracelets carve *Have Faith*... and, on the other, *I Will Wait on You*," I instructed.

It turned out perfect. The hot nail pressed Jimmy's handwriting into the leather flawlessly. Jimmy put the bracelets back in the box and I shoved them in my backpack. He extended his hand, but I gave him a hug. "Thank you," I said, as I headed for the door.

"No, thank you, Joseph. Thank you for having the courage I didn't," he said, with a weak smile.

Next, I rode my bike to Sarah's place. She answered the door. I explained my predicament and tried to apologize for the night before, but she interrupted me with a hug.

"Joseph, I'm so embarrassed. I was so out of line. I don't know what I was thinking. Can you ever forgive me?" she asked, humbly.

"I have nothing to forgive you for."

"You are the best, Joseph. I meant every word I said last night. Accept for the crazy stuff," she laughed.

"I wouldn't call it crazy. To be honest, I'm flattered," I said, sincerely.

Sarah asked, "Can you do me a favor before you go?"

"Anything. What do you need?" I said.

Sarah looked in both directions, to make sure we weren't being watched. She grabbed me by my cheeks, pulled my head in close, and kissed me. Her lips were soft. Guard down, I surrendered to her will. We stood there for what seemed like forever. And honestly, I didn't want it to end.

With flushed cheeks and a fluttering heart, I said, "So that's what that feels like?"

"That's why I love you Joseph. Don't lose yourself in Seattle. You're perfect," she said, with a gleam in her eyes.

Sarah let me come to say my goodbyes to Pastor Paul and Papa Pete. They were enjoying lunch after the morning church service. They wished me well and prayed for my safe journey.

From there, I went to Little PJ's place. He was weak from vomiting all night. I told him about what happened between me and Duke. He was excited and a little jealous of my early departure.

I assured him, "I'll find a nice place for us and cover the rent until you get there."

"I'll be there in September. You better not have a bunch of fun without me."

"I won't, I promise," I said, definitely.

Little PJ hugged me. I could tell that he didn't want to let me go. I didn't want to let go either. He buried his face in my chest and cried. He squeezed me as tight as he could. I couldn't help but cry, too.

I said, "It's going to be OK. I promise I won't do anything without you. You are my best friend and we are going to do everything together."

He sobbed, "It's not that. I remember how my life was before we were friends. I don't know if I can make it without you. I can't make it without you, Joseph." His words were muffled by my shirt.

"Look at me, Little PJ. Please look at me." He wiped his eyes. His face was red and flush. I asked, "Do you remember when you grabbed that mop in O'Dell's and stood up against the entire football team?"

"Yeah, I remember."

"I was scared out of my mind. Then, my best friend stepped in. You faced my giants, Little PJ. And they backed down. You're greater than you know. One day, you're going to change the world. You've already changed mine. If anyone should be worried about being alone, it's me."

"Don't make another best friend. I'm your best friend. Just don't forget that," he asserted.

"That isn't even possible. You will always be my best friend. I'll call you as soon as I get a place."

It was time for my most difficult farewell. I had to part ways with Mrs. Kat. In a strange way, I felt like she was my responsibility. Who was going to take care of her? How would she manage? I guess there was only so much I could do. I'd have her give Meadow the bracelet for me.

I arrived at Mrs. Kat's house and took everything in. I looked at the perfectly manicured yard, the freshly painted fence, the lacquered porch, and I reminisced. There was love in this work.

Mrs. Kat answered the door and said, "Come on in, Joseph."

"Mrs. Kat, I just came over to say good bye. I'm going off to Seattle a little earlier than I thought."

"When are you leaving?" she asked, sadly.

"I'm leaving tonight. I just wanted to come and tell you that I love you and that I'll miss you. And that I will visit every summer."

She said, "You've been really good to me. I probably haven't shown it in the best way. But I hope you know that I appreciate everything you've done."

"The pleasure was all mine, Mrs. Kat. Do you mind giving something to Meadow for me?"

"Why don't you give it to her yourself? She's in her room. But I doubt she will let you in. Her new boyfriend worked her face over something good."

My heart sank. I knew that Mrs. Kat was telling the truth. I thought to myself, 'Why would she let someone treat her like that?'

I knocked on Meadow's door.

"Go away!" She must have assumed I was her mother.

"Meadow, it's me, Joseph. Are you OK?"

"I'm OK. What are you doing here?" she asked.

"I'm here to say goodbye. I'm leaving for school. I have a gift for you. Come out of there so I can see you before I go."

"No... I mean... I can't let you see me like this. Just leave it on the table."

"OK," I responded, disappointedly.

"I'm so excited for you, JoJo. You're finally getting out of this stupid town."

"Maybe you can come visit," I said, hopefully.

"Big cities have a knack for changing people. You'll probably meet some cute daddy's girl," she said, with sass.

"I won't," I giggled.

"Take care, JoJo."

"I will, Meadow."

I took a few steps toward the front door. Then I turned around. I almost forgot to give Meadow a message. I walked back to Meadow's door and gently tapped on its rough surface.

"Yes, Joseph?"

"How did you know it was me?"

"I just knew."

"I almost forgot to tell you something."

"What's that?"

"Have faith... I will wait on you."

I listened for a response. But she stayed silent. On the coffee table, I placed the bracelet that said, *Have Faith...* I left a note next to it that read:

Wear this, and know that I will always wait on you.

Love,

JoJo

Mrs. Kat stopped me before I could leave. I embraced her and she broke down in my arms. I could feel her tears on my neck. She whispered into my ear, "Joseph, I am a horrible person..."

I interrupted, "No you aren't, Mrs. Kat, it's just the alcohol talking."

Something almost mystical came over her as she spoke. "Shhhh... I need you to be quite and listen for a moment. Really listen, Joseph. I am a horrible person for what I'm about to say. I should be telling you to leave and never come back. You are like an angel, locked up in the dark. You're the only light in a sea of nothingness. Your light is wonderful and gorgeous. But, that light attracts the rats, roaches, and parasites. All of them are attracted to you. You are life and hope to them. Of course they want to be close to you! But, if you stay around the infested long enough, their filth will rub off on you. Their young will eat at your garment, their dirt will matte your wings, and their disease will blind you. Me and my daughter, we are parasites, Joseph. You're better than us. Stick around long enough and we will destroy you."

"But, Mrs. Kat..."

"Hush, Joseph. I haven't got to why I'm a horrible person. I'm a selfish and horrible person because I'm not going to tell you to escape, and leave this place for good. Instead, I'm going to beg you to come back for my daughter. You are the only person that can save her. I knew it the first time I met you. I recognized it when you paid for my furnace."

"You knew?" I asked, shocked.

"Of course I knew. Remember, I'm a parasite, and parasites recognize light... we recognize life giving sources. I wasn't always like this, but I know what I've become. Please, find a way to save her! Not for her, not even for yourself, but for me. Help me make up for the horrible mistakes I made as a mother. I'm counting on you to mend my daughter and put yourself at risk, in the process. And that is why I'm a horrible person."

I broke our embrace. And, for the first time, I had nothing to say to Mrs. Kat. She had shared more honesty then I could digest.

I made my way to my last stop before Seattle. I visited my grand-father's grave and paid my last respects.

I arrived at the bus station around 7:00pm. I had some time before my departure. I decided to reflect and say a small prayer:

Please, watch over the people I love. Protect and care for them while I'm gone.

Chapter 14
Finished Before I Could Start

S eattle stirred something inside me I didn't know existed. I found new inspiration, a fresh outlook on how I viewed myself and everything around me. The concrete streets and sidewalks supported a steady flow of people, love, life, and potential. And choice was the name of the game. There was a diversity of culture, activities, and ideas. I was smack-dab between all of them. I loved every minute of it.

There were a few religious people in my town that warned me of the wiles of the city. They told me to beware; the city had junctions and burrows where God refused to abide. They warned me against losing myself in the hypnotic glow of bright lights and the seductive allure of independence. I gave their advice some consideration. But I learned, long ago, not to put weight in hearsay. For I had not met the metropolis they had described. I had never seen buildings so tall, opportunities so abundant, and so many people chasing a dream. I was in Meadow's town, a collection of communities pregnant with expectation. It didn't take long to find a place to stay. It took even less time to make Seattle my home.

I moved into a home in the perfect location. The landlords, John and Chris Parton, owned a quaint townhome a few blocks from Seattle University. There was a bus stop a block away. The route ran to UW.

The two, retired lovebirds decided to rent out the basement of their house. And, since I had lived in a basement my entire life, the Parton residence felt like home. I found the place by scouring the classified ads. The article read, *Retired pastor and wife renting a quiet space next to Seattle University.* They were hoping potential renters read between the lines. What they were really saying was: "We have a room... no riffraff allowed."

I called them right away. I explained to Mr. Parton that I was going to school to be a journalist and that Little PJ would be attending Seattle University in the fall. He said, "Son, you sound like you have a good head on your shoulders. Why don't you meet me at my house for lunch?"

"That sounds great. What day and time work for you?" I asked.

"How about tomorrow around noon?"

I stayed a couple of nights in a motel, and I couldn't wait to move into a real place. The Partons and I hit it off from the start. They were like the parents I never had. At first, Mr. Parton was a bit uncomfortable renting to me. I hadn't secured a job and I had no local references. I put all his concerns to rest when I handed him an envelope with three months' rent in advance.

Finding a job was trickier than finding a place to hang my hat. I dropped off my resume at every diner in the city. The timing wasn't ideal. Most of the positions were taken by students that had worked at the establishments for years, or by those that applied in spring.

It was mid-July. I had just left the thousandth place that wasn't hiring. Fed up, I decided to walk it off. Mr. and Mrs. Parton had been so good to me. The last thing that I wanted to do was come home with an attitude.

I strolled along the broken sidewalks until I reached downtown Seattle. I walked past a fancy restaurant that I would have normally ignored. It was one of those places where the city's upper crust went for happy hour. A country boy like me would have stuck out like a sore thumb. But I wasn't drawn to the fresh, white linen that laid over the table rounds, the perfectly executed mood lighting, the mahogany wood molding, or the red and gold wallpaper that added a regal feel to the space. I was attracted to a sign that read, *Considering Qualified Help.*

This was the first place that was actually hiring. I thought about going home to change. I didn't look presentable enough to step into an establishment like that. But then I thought to myself, 'What if I went home and they filled the position?' No... I needed to go in and apply now. I took a deep breath and walked through the restaurant doors. Within seconds, I was greeted by the maître d'. He was a good-looking man with impeccable taste. He sized me up.

"Do you have a reservation Sir?" he asked, in a discriminating tone.

"No sir. I am here to apply for a job."

"The position has been filled," he scoffed. I almost walked out. But I had come too far to let this judgmental gatekeeper get in the way of an opportunity. If I was going to get turned down, it would come from the top.

"May I speak to your manager?" I asked, politely.

"Excuse me?" he asked, annoyed.

"May I speak to your manager, please?"

The maître d' gave a brief nod and disappeared into the back. A few minutes went by before he returned with another man. He was just as sharp as the maître d', but he had a sparkle in his eye and joy in his step. He looked at me, and extended his hand.

"My name is Tim Lasso, and your name is?"

"Joseph O'Dell, sir."

"Reginald said that you would like to speak to me. How can I assist you?"

"I would like to speak to you about your position for hire," I said, confidently.

"Sure, follow me."

Reginald gave me the evil eye as we walked past him. We made our way to the back of the restaurant, and took a seat at a booth near the kitchen. I set my backpack down, unzipped it, and went for my résumé.

"Joseph, I don't need your résumé."

"How did you know what I was grabbing for?"

"Let's just say that I've done this a time or two. This is your official interview and I only have one question. Are you ready for the question?"

I got nervous. But, before the butterflies could take flight, I said to myself, 'You are supposed to be here. This interview happened for a reason. You are supposed to be here, Joseph.' And then added, aloud, "I'm ready for your question, Mr. Lasso."

He picked up a carafe of water that was sitting on the table. He poured himself a glass of water and took a sip. He looked me directly in the eyes and said, "Many manage... I lead. What is the difference?"

The question perplexed me at first. I thought to myself, 'What is the difference between a manager and a leader?' I thought about the people in my life. Duke was a solid example of a manager. He knew how to boss me around and make sure that O'Dell's had what it needed to keep the doors open. I also knew true leaders. People like Burm, Pastor Paul, Papa Pete, and Sarah. They knew how to get the job done while bringing out the best in people.

I cleared my throat and said, "Mr. Lasso, do you mind if I have some time to answer the question? And if you don't mind, I would like to write the answer down on paper."

Mr. Lasso wore an amused smirk, took another sip of water, and said, "Son, this is an interview. Part of interviewing is testing how you think on your feet. It is also a test of your oral skills. So, why should I give you more time to answer the question, and why should I let you write it down? After all, this isn't a final exam, this is an opportunity for employment."

I paused to organize my thoughts before I spoke. I wanted my words to mean something.

I said, "I'm sure you've sat in front of a lot of people that have impressed you by saying the right things. But, in time, you realize that what they say and what they do don't add up. Like you said when we first met, you've done this a time or two."

"Go on... I'm interested," he said, with a smile.

"Interviewing is like a first date. Each person tries to overwhelm the other with their strengths in hopes that they won't notice their weaknesses. I have no intention of carrying on a honeymoon stage with you. I want to be very transparent about who I am and what I can offer, both good and bad. I am a better writer than speaker. And I would rather take the time to write down how I really feel about your question versus quickly telling you what I think you want to hear. If you like the answer, maybe you could give me a shot. And if you don't like it... well, then I will apologize for wasting your time."

"I like you, kid. Fair enough. I will be back in 20 minutes."

I took my notebook and pen out of my backpack. At the top of a piece of paper I wrote, *Many Manage... I Lead.* There is a huge difference between two. I realized what Mr. Lasso was getting at.

20 minutes passed, and Mr. Lasso sat back down at the table.
"So, are you finished?" he asked.
"Yes. And thank you for giving me the time," I said, gratefully.
"Do you mind if I read your answer aloud, Joseph?"
"I don't mind at all."
I passed him my notebook and he read:

Many Manage... I Lead

There are many managers
Overseers of people, projects, departments, and divisions
I don't consider myself a manager
I've made a career of providing vision

I don't get caught up in taking credit
Or putting my selfish interest before the team
On the contrary, I've accepted a position of service
I'm most ambitious when assisting them to attain their dreams

I consistently set clear expectations
Then I trust my team enough to give them space
If they fall short of their objectives
I've learned that anyone can chastise, but it
takes a greater person to exercise grace

I know my people and leverage their strengths
With every task I make them aware of their significance
If I drop the ball or push them beyond their abilities
It is my job to fill in the deficit

I'm surprised at how low people stoop
To advance in their lonely careers
Growing people is a privilege
I hope that everyone I impact, will one day become my peer

Leadership requires courage under fire
To execute when you want to stay frozen
It's not something to be dabbled in, not for the faint of heart
Many are called but few are chosen

I'm a builder of dreams
An arrestor of insecurities
I'm a filler of needs
For my team, I bleed

And they will stand with me in the 11th hour
Because, I made sure they were empowered
For me, they will walk through fire
Because, I'm just as passionate about their desires

If things get confused
Or somewhat unstable
I strip off my badge
And consult our round table

When the winds howl and the waters rise
When faith begins to slip
That's when we're the closest; I'd never abandon them
I'd rather go down with this ship.

It's my job to see you pass me
It's my job to see you outlast me
It's my job to keep you in the know
It's my job to see that you grow

Many want to see a harvest without planting the necessary seed

Many Manage... I Lead.

Mr. Lasso put down the notebook and clapped his hands together. "Bravo... Bravo, Joseph."

It took everything in my power not to blush.

"Joseph, you were right. Most people try to answer that question as quickly as possible. They tell me what they think I want to hear. Only two other people in my entire career have asked for time to think about the question. Both of those people have gone on to do greater things. They took advantage of opportunities that this place couldn't even come close to offering. But Joseph, no one, and I mean no one, has answered the question like this. Do you mind if I keep this? I want to frame it and put it in my office. I have a feeling that you are going to do something special someday."

"Thank you, sir. You can have it. I just need to make a copy. I always keep a copy of my writings."

I copied it word for word while he sat there. He had a look of bewilderment on his face.

"Where did you come from?" he asked, astonished.

"I'm from a small town in Central Washington."

"You're a diamond in the rough... that's what you are... a diamond in the rough. How would you like to work for me?"

"When can I start?" I asked, excitedly.

"How about tomorrow?"

"Tomorrow works for me."

I was promoted three times in two months. I eventually took Reginald's job. I rubbed shoulders with professional athletes, government officials, the occasional movie star visiting the northwest, socialites, and the upper echelon of the business community. Mr. Lasso warned me of the allure of celebrity. He said it would change me for the worse, if I let it. So, I tried to remain true to myself, and I looked to add value everywhere. I didn't wait for Tim to ask me to do something. When I was done with one task I moved on to the next. I guess I could thank Duke for that much.

The middle of September rolled around in no time. It was a Friday afternoon when Little PJ finally arrived. He couldn't believe what I had accomplished in such little time. I was off that night, so I treated him to a meal at the restaurant.

With a full heart and a huge grin, Little PJ said, "Joseph, we are going to do something big together. I can just feel it."

He was under the big city's spell too. After eating, we went down to the pier. The sun barely peaked over the horizon. The sky was painted soft yellows and oranges. We had come so far. For the first time in our lives, Little PJ and I were free. I couldn't wait to start school on Monday and neither could Little PJ. We took a bus back to the Parton home and caught up.

Monday came around, and Little PJ and I got up together. It was time to start chipping away at our purpose. We were so excited that neither one of us could sleep the night before. We got dressed, ate breakfast, and headed in opposite directions for our respective schools.

When I arrived to campus, I was met by news that would change my life for good. I walked into my first class. I noticed that the blackboard read, *Joseph O'Dell, see the counselor right away.*

I went up to the instructor and said, "Hi, I'm Joseph O'Dell. Can you tell me what this note is about?" The instructor couldn't give me any information. He advised me to see the counselor ASAP. When I arrived, I was given a note to call home. I thought to myself, 'What could have happened?' I tried my best not to panic. The counselor gave me a phone and some privacy. I called the shop, but there was no answer. Why wasn't Duke picking up the phone during business hours? I called home.

"Hello."

"Mom... what's going on? Is everything OK?" I panicked.

"Joseph, you need to get home now! You're father had a massive stroke. And I can't take care of him."

"What do you mean take care of him?" I asked, puzzled.

"He is having trouble speaking and he can barely get around the house. It serves him right. I'm not taking care of that man and I refuse to set foot in his shop," she said, hatefully.

"Mom, I know that you haven't got along but..."

My mother interrupted and lashed out ferociously, "Who do you think you're talking to, Joseph O'Dell?" Once sparked, Gloria's anger was fierce. "So, you think you're all grown up now? You don't have a clue. Get home now... NOW!"

Click

I fantasized about ignoring my mother's phone call. What was the worst that could happen? They weren't my responsibility. They were the parents! Why should I sacrifice my happiness for them? They didn't care about me, so why should I care for them?

My thoughts sobered quickly. Already, my heart knew the right answer. I had to accept the inevitable. I was finished before I started.

My heart sank at what I knew I had to do – what I had to leave behind. I wanted to write stories that helped people. But my efforts would be hypocritical if I turned my back on my parents. I had gone above and beyond for everyone else. What kind of person would I be if I couldn't show them the same consideration?

I took a bus down to the restaurant to put in my notice. I had to tell Tim in person. He must have read the despair on my face.

"You have to leave. I understand, Joseph," he said, sincerely.

"How did you know I had to leave?" I asked, curiously.

"Like I said before, I've done this a time or two."

"I can't begin to repay you for what you've done for me, Mr. Lasso. I will be back one day."

"Joseph, I hope you won't. You're going to do big things, kid. Take care of yourself. And let me know if there is anything that I can do for you in the future."

"There is one thing. I have a friend. He's a freshman at Seattle University. We grew up together. He's like family. If he comes here for help, all I ask is that you consider his request. His name is Little PJ."

"Not a problem, Joseph. If he's family to you, he's family to us." Tim gave me a firm handshake that turned into a hug before we parted ways.

I went back to the Parton's home and explained my situation. I gave John another two months' rent in advance. It was a buffer for Little PJ. It might take him some time to find a roommate.

Mr. Parton said, "You're something really special. God has his hand on your life. I give you my word, even if Little PJ can't find a roommate, we will forgive half of the rent for as long as he stays."

"I appreciate it, Mr. Parton," I said, gratefully.

I went downstairs to pack my stuff and prepare for my conversation with Little PJ. How would I tell him that we weren't going to do this part of life together? I was sick to my stomach. I didn't want to hurt my best friend, but I needed to leave. My mother wouldn't survive the stress.

A couple of hours went by, and Little PJ came home. He trampled down the stairs and saw me sitting on my freshly made bed next to neatly packed bags. "What happened?" he asked, surprised. I took my time answering. I needed to be strong, and I didn't want to cry.

I muttered, "Duke had a stroke. He can't speak too well, and he's having a tough time getting around. I spoke with my mother a couple of times today and she is having a nervous breakdown. She's already depressed but this... this will kill her. She doesn't want to take care of him and she doesn't know the first thing about running the shop. Little PJ, I have to go home."

He stared at me for a moment. Then he grabbed his suitcase from beneath his bed. He placed it on his mattress and began to stuff his belongings into it.

"What do you think you're doing?" I shouted.

"I can't let you do this by yourself, Joseph. I'm going with you," he said, determined.

"No, you're not!!!"

I scurried over to him and grabbed his stuff out of his suitcase. He pushed my hands away and started putting it back in. That's when I grabbed his suitcase and threw it across the room. Instinctively, Little PJ pushed me.

"What the hell are you doing?" he yelled.

I couldn't keep the tears from coming. I loved Little PJ so much. I wouldn't let him jeopardize his future. "I can't let you do this, Little PJ. As a matter of fact, I won't let you. If you try to follow me back home... I... I... I will never speak to you again. Our friendship would be over. This is my fight, not yours. Do you understand me...? Do you understand me?!"

"No, I don't understand you, Joseph, and I don't understand why everything happens to you. You are the nicest person I know, but you never get a break. I'm so tired of it. If it was my parents that were sick, you'd go back with me in a heartbeat. Wouldn't you, Joseph?" he shrilled.

"Yes," I admitted.

"So how can you expect me to stay?" he cried.

"You have to stay because some opportunities don't come around again. You have an opportunity to do what no one in your family has done. You can show them that getting your education is the right thing to do. You can end the poverty in your family. Little PJ, you can still make your parents proud. That's something I'll never be able to do, no matter what. But that doesn't mean they aren't my responsibility. They are MY responsibility, not yours."

"But Joseph, you know this isn't right. Why don't you just live for yourself, here, with me? I'm sure that your parents will figure it out – they're adults. You've come this far, why turn back now?"

"Because I have faith that if I do the right things, one day, everything will work out for good. Everything in my body wants to stay and enjoy myself for once in my life. But that would be the easy way out. I wouldn't be able to live with myself if I acted so selfishly. My mother asked for my help. I need to go home."

Little PJ quietly let my words soak in for a few moments.

"Joseph, I will come and visit you winter break."

"No you won't. I don't want you to come back until you are done. You are not to see me for four years."

"But why?" he asked, bewildered.

"It's just better that way. I know how our town is. There is something about it. If you come back, you will find an excuse to stay. I've paid up the rent for another two months. Also, if you ever need work, or get in a bind, go see Tim Lasso. He is a friend and he will help. You can do this on your own, Little PJ."

"I'll make you proud, Joseph," he promised.

The bus ride home was long and uncomfortable. I finally understood what Mrs. Kat warned me of. I was light in a dark place. I was food for the parasites.

Seeing Seattle in the rearview was a sad sight. And going back home brought about even stranger feelings. As I settled in, I wrote to pass the time.

Empty Bus

Dirty polyester and insignificant patterns
Cover this uncomfortable seat
Can't find the positive, my thoughts scattered
While surrounded by a looming sense of defeat

I'm sure that many have sat on this very bus
Running from their own version of hell
You failure, misfit, freak
Allegations they try to dispel

Head rested against a window, covered in dry tears
Some of them my own
Most people run from shameful places and fear
Yet, I find myself going home

Stopping in the places rarely noticed
God-forsaken towns where the tumbleweeds still roll
No time for dreams, no need for focus
Maybe I'll shelve them, put these precious things on hold

I look inside for a courage I cannot hone
It's the right thing to do, but I struggle to trust it
I can't help but notice that I'm all alone
Only fools ride on empty busses

I could only stay in this melancholy mood for so long. I had an entire bus ride to put my attitude in check. If I did not approach this challenge with the right spirit, it would own me. I refused to let that happen.

I walked through the doors of my house. It already seemed like so much had changed. Duke was sitting on the couch in the living room. I could see drool spots on his shirt. This was not the same man I left. My mother came down the stairs.

"I wasn't sure you were going to come back."

"You said you needed my help, mom. So I'm here."

"There's a list of things he needs and a schedule of his doctor's appointments on the kitchen table. His keys are hanging up by the door." My father had tons of useless keys on a giant key ring. My mother turned around and began her ascent back up the stairs.

"Wait a minute. That's it? You just give me a to-do list and that's it? I put my life on hold and all I get is a to-do list? You didn't even ask me how my trip was," I said, frustrated.

"Joseph, just deal with your father and make sure to keep the shop running. I will do my part when you're working. Otherwise, he's your problem," she snapped. I couldn't believe the bitterness spewing from Gloria's mouth.

"What did he do to hurt you so bad?" I asked. Insulted by my question, Gloria walked up the stairs and into her room. She slammed the door behind her.

I felt horrible for Duke. All I could think about was the fact that the last, real conversation we had, involved me telling him that I hated him. I would spend the rest of my life making it up to him. I started by making him dinner.

I made my father some mashed potatoes and gravy. I assisted him in eating his meal. Most of the food dribbled down his chin. But I scooped it back up, and fed him again. After a tedious dinner, I put him to bed. It was like taking care of a child. The experience absolutely broke my heart. It was overwhelming. I needed to get out of this house. Maybe Mrs. Kat was up. I knew it was a long shot, but maybe Meadow was home, too.

Mrs. Kat's house had almost gone back to its original state. The porch was cluttered, the grass had grown out of control, and a spirit of despair loomed over the entire property again.

I knocked on the door. Mrs. Kat invited me in, but there was no Meadow. She met a guy at a club. Meadow decided to follow him to Los Angeles. He had supposed connections in Hollywood, and was going to help Meadow become a star. Mrs. Kat was beside herself. I assured her that Meadow would be back. I had a long road ahead of myself. But I would make it.

"Mr. Joseph, did you ever think that you were a little too nice? Maybe, Little PJ was right... maybe you should have stayed in Seattle. There's nothing wrong with looking out for yourself."

"Bridgett Marie, you're right. There's nothing wrong with putting yourself first. But at what cost? What if my father died due to lack of care? What if my mother lost the shop and her home? Would my happiness be worth it?"

She said, "I didn't think of it that way. Now I feel stupid for opening up my big mouth."

I grabbed her by the hand and said, "You are right to feel the way you do. There is nothing stupid about it. Try to look at it like this. There's an old saying, it goes, 'With great power comes great responsibility.' If this is true, then the inverse must be true, also. When we take on responsibility, we become powerful. I didn't know it at the time, but I won my freedom when I got on that bus. Real freedom takes place when we have a choice to make. I chose the responsibility of my family. I chose to be powerful."

Chapter 15

Pleasant Surprise

A year went by. I grew accustomed to my new routine. My life re-volved around the shop, Duke, and Mrs. Kat, in that order. But I didn't do it alone. I had the support of Pastor Paul, Papa Pete, Jimmy, and other community members that frequented O'Dell's. Their help was invaluable. Every day, a different person found an excuse to come and encourage me. It was nice.

One Saturday evening, the shop bell rang announcing the arrival of two of my favorite supporters, Pastor Paul and Papa Pete. "How can I help you troublemakers?" I greeted them.

Pastor Paul said, "We're looking for motivation for tomorrow's message."

"I don't know how much motivation you two are going to find in a creamery," I teased.

Papa Pete responded, "You'd be surprised."

Pastor Paul asked, "By the way, how is Duke?"

"He's does a little better every day. He gets frustrated. I don't think things are moving along quick enough for him."

"How about you, Joseph, how are you doing?" Papa Pete asked.

"I'm doing well. I've got into a bit of a routine. I'm waiting for the opportunity to go back to school. But in the meantime, I'm not complaining. I'm grateful for what I have."

Pastor Paul looked at me like a light bulb turned on and said, "Joseph, I have to go. The inspiration came and I need to write it down before it leaves."

"No problem, Pastor Paul. I'll see you later."

"What will it be for you tonight, Papa Pete? It's on the house."

"A couple of scoops of strawberry will be fine. Come and sit with me while I eat." The shop was pretty dead, so I didn't see any harm. "You know, I'm so proud of you Joseph."

"I'm just doing what I have to do, that's all," I responded, humbly.

"I understand. But most people, especially your age, would have cracked under the pressure. I have to say, I'm touched, and very impressed."

"Can I be honest about something, Papa Pete?"

"Yes. Anything."

"I'm sort of disappointed with my life. I feel like I'm stuck and have no control. I want to get out of here and make a real difference. But instead, I serve ice cream all day."

"Joseph, you don't have to be a journalist, corporate big-shot, or even a pastor to make a difference. Greatness is not a destination. It is a state of mind. You have the ability to affect thousands of people, just doing what you do every day."

"And how is that?" I asked.

"It's not what you do, but the spirit in which you do it. You're not just serving up ice cream. You're scooping up hope. Believe it or not, you're already making a difference." Papa Pete got up from the table and took his ice cream to go. He shook my hand. "I'll have to tell you how Pastor Paul and I met some day."

I prepped the shop for closing, when an unexpected visitor showed up. It was Sarah. She was in her sophomore year at Central Washington. But she still lived at home. I would see her from time to time between midterms and finals. But most of the time, she just buried herself in her studies.

"Hey, ice cream man, what are you up to?" she asked, with a smile.

"Nothing much. You just missed your dad."

"I know. He said he was coming down here for inspiration, and suddenly I was in the mood for a sundae. Hot fudge is my inspiration," she teased.

"One hot fudge sundae coming right up." I took my time making Sarah's sundae. By the time I was done with it, it looked more like art than a dessert.

"Come and sit with me, Joseph."

I went to the front door, flipped the open sign to the closed side, and locked the door. I couldn't help but stare at her. It still surprised me how this tomboy had transformed into this beautiful princess that sat in my booth. She spooned a couple of bites into her mouth.

"What are you doing Sunday night?" she asked.

"I will be helping Mrs. Kat out until supper time. I told her that I would pressure wash her mossy roof. But I should be done around 7:00pm."

She twirled her fudge-stained spoon between her fingers and asked, "Do you want to hang out after you're done? It seems like neither one of us has had much of a break lately."

"Are you sure you want to slum it with me? There are plenty of college guys that would probably make for better company," I teased.

"None of those guys come close to you, Joseph. And I'm not just saying that." Her compliment made me smile. "Plus, I want to catch-up with an old friend. Is that a crime?" she asked.

"OK. You're right. I will meet you here around 8:00pm. That will give me enough time to get cleaned up."

"It's a date, Joseph."

"It's a date," I agreed.

Sarah finished her sundae and left. I wiped down the counters and mopped the floors. The shop was closed on Sunday and I didn't want to come back to a mess on Monday. I learned to be really efficient. I was no longer assisting Duke; I ran the place solo. After finishing my chores, I turned out the lights, and headed for the shop door. I was just about to turn the knob when the phone rang. I figured I better answer it. It may have been an emergency. I made my way through the dark creamery.

"O'Dell's Creamery. This is Joseph, how can I help you?"

"Hey, Joseph. It's Kat."

"Hey, Mrs. Kat. Is everything OK?"

She had a zest in her voice that I had never heard. Something exciting was going on. "Everything is perfect. Meadow came home. You need to come over right away. My baby is home!!!"

"I'll be right over," I said, in shock.

I hung up the phone, and I felt my heart skip a beat. Meadow had been gone a little over a year. There were days when I doubted if I would see her again. I was so excited I could hardly stand it. I tripped over a chair as I skipped through the dark shop. I put the chair back and escaped through the front door. 'Wait... I almost forgot,' I thought to myself. I went back into the shop and scooped up a to-go carton of pralines n' cream.

I smiled from ear to ear all the way to her house. I smiled so hard that my cheeks were sore by the time I got there. I had been to this house hundreds of times, but Meadow's return made me feel like a stranger on its premises. It felt like a first date.

I knocked on the door and Meadow answered. We stared at each other for what seemed like forever. Once I broke her trance, I was riddled with concern. Meadow's eyes were puffy and dark. She had lost a good 15 pounds, and her skin was blotchy. Her time away had been rough. It was bad enough for her to run home.

Meadow embraced me and said, "I missed you, JoJo."

"I missed you too, Meadow. I brought you something." I pulled the carton of pralines n' cream out of my backpack.

"It's your favorite," I said.

"You are so sweet. Come in."

Mrs. Kat almost tackled me.

"Can you believe she came home, Joseph? I'm still in shock," she ranted, through tears.

"It's a great surprise, Mrs. Kat. So what have you girls been up to?"

"We just had some dinner. My mom made meatloaf. There's some leftovers if you want it," Meadow giggled, and then winked. She knew I absolutely despised meatloaf. To top it off, Mrs. Kat wasn't the best cook. I was in double trouble.

"I'll pass... I mean... I ate at the shop and I'm still full."

"What, my mother's cooking isn't good enough for you?" Meadow teased.

"Yeah... my cooking isn't good enough for you?" Mrs. Kat chimed in. I couldn't believe that Meadow was trying to set me up. She held her hand over her mouth trying not to laugh out loud. I grabbed Mrs. Kat by the hand.

I announced, "Beautiful, you know I love your cooking. I'm just stuffed."

"Flattery will get you nowhere. Its OK, I'm tired. I think I'm going to go to bed and let you two catch-up."

Meadow sat on the couch with JoJo the bear. I couldn't believe she still had it. I sat next to her and she grabbed my hand.

"Why are you so good to my mother? She hasn't stopped talking about you since I got home. Everything was 'Joseph this' and 'Joseph that.' You might be her favorite person in the world. I'm not sure if I've told you, and shame on me if I haven't, but thank you. Thank you for taking care of my mother. We really don't deserve you."

"You two are like family to me. And that means there is no getting rid of me," I joked.

"You have kinda stuck around," Meadow laughed.

"In all seriousness, I'm happy to help. I love..." I stopped, realizing that I might be opening up an inappropriate conversation. I looked away in embarrassment. Meadow, sensing I was somewhat embarrassed, finished my sentence.

"I love you too, JoJo." Things got uncomfortably quiet for a moment, so I took the initiative to change the subject.

"How are things going in California? I want to hear about every-thing." Meadow looked away. Her facial expressions changed, as if I had opened up some painful box of memories. Sensing that I was mak-ing her uncomfortable, I tried changing the subject again. "Meadow, we don't have to get into California if you don't want to. We can talk about something else."

She manufactured a smile and said, "No it's fine. Things are going great. I've been promised to star in some movies and a few commercials. Things couldn't be better, JoJo. I'm on the verge of my big break."

Her words said one thing, but her body language told a different story. But, who was I to judge? I had fallen short of my dreams as well. Besides, none of that mattered to me. Her safe return home was the important thing.

I went to the kitchen and cleaned up. I couldn't help it. It was a habit. "What are you doing?" she asked.

"I'm just straightening up."

"I can get to that later. I'm in the mood for a walk. Do you mind?"

"I'm up for anything."

"I have to keep my figure up for all those casting calls," she giggled. We held hands as we made our way to the sidewalk.

"Where would you like to go?" I asked.

"I don't know. Let's just walk until we come across something interesting enough to stop."

"That's one of the things that I love about you. I might even be a little envious," I explained.

"What do you mean?" she asked.

"I love how free you are. You just take every day... every moment, as it comes. You're not like me, always planning... Mr. Predictable."

"My freedom comes at a cost. Trust me, JoJo, I'm not as free as you think," she said, sadly.

We took turns making small talk. Before I knew it, we were downtown, in front of O'Dell's. Meadow stopped walking.

"Why would you stop here? What is so interesting about this place?" I asked, curiously.

"I remember the first day I walked through those doors. You were so nervous. Do you remember?"

"Unfortunately, yes," I admitted.

"Joseph, you have changed in all the right ways. You have so much more confidence; yet, you've kept the same heart. I just don't know how you do it." Meadow moved a few steps closer to me. We were inches away from each other. She grabbed both of my hands with hers and gently swung my arms from left to right. "You have a bracelet, too?" The swinging had exposed my bracelet underneath my sleeve.

"I do. Read what it says."

Meadow pulled my wrist up to her face and read, *I Will Wait on You.*

"It's a promise I will never break," I said, sincerely. She pulled up her left sleeve. She had her bracelet on, too. Somehow, it made me feel better. Maybe it was a silly way to think, but knowing that she wore the bracelet, gave me hope.

Meadow said, "You are growing up to be very handsome. I'm surprised you aren't married yet. Isn't that how you small town boys do it? You marry the girl next door and have a ton of kids. You're 20, right?"

"Yes."

"You should have 3 kids by now, and be working on your fourth," she teased. I laughed at her ridiculous comments.

"I'm not waiting on the girl next door. I'm waiting on THE GIRL."

"Oh really, what is this girl like?" she asked flirtatiously.

"Well, she's sort of a puzzle."

"Do tell," she said, with a grin.

"Most people are attracted to her looks, but that is just the tip of the iceberg. Her beauty begins within. She has the strength to move mountains, but somewhere along the way, she convinced herself otherwise. She has too much talent and potential for a small town like this. She searches for significance, and in the process, has forgotten that she is already great. She's fragile, but mighty. She stops space and time."

"I wish I could be half the girl you make me out to be."

"Who said I was talking about you?" I joked.

Meadow hit me on the shoulder and said, "How rude! You better be talking about me."

I giggled as she struck me on the shoulder again. I stopped her swings and embraced her. After holding her for a few seconds longer than I probably should have, I looked expectantly into her weak eyes. "Meadow, I have something that I need to tell you."

"I already know what you are going to say. You say it every time we part."

"You don't know what I'm about to say," I challenged. Meadow crossed her arms and shifted her weight to her right hip. She wore a big smirk across her beautiful face.

She said, "I'll make you a deal. If I can guess what you were about to say, then I will never leave this dingy town again. And, if I get it wrong... well then you owe me a thousand orders of pralines n' cream."

"Wait Meadow, that bet is backwards. Shouldn't it be the other way around?"

"No, the bet is perfect the way it is. Do you accept?"

"I accept."

"In the sweetest voice, you were going to say, 'Have faith... I will wait on you.'"

I shook my head from side to side. "I guess I'm going to owe you a lot of ice cream."

Meadow's face got really serious. In a concerned voice, she said, "You weren't going to tell me that?"

I couldn't hold a straight face. "Of course I was," I laughed.

"I guess, that means that I'm staying," she said, with a smile.

"That's fine by me."

Meadow hugged me tightly, and then whispered into my ear, "Do you want to open up the shop for us?"

"Did you want something to eat?" I asked, naively.

"No, silly, I never got to officially thank you for what you've done for me and my mom." Suddenly, I read between the lines and my nerves kicked in.

I stammered, "Meadow, what are you trying to say?"

"I just figure we could fool around and see where it goes."

Meadow placed her pouty lips on the edge of my mouth, kissing more lips than cheek. She placed one hand on my face and used the other to rub the small of my back. The urge to kiss her back and take her into the empty shop was almost uncontrollable. But... I couldn't, not like this. Meadow wanted to give herself out of obligation. Her experiences had conditioned her to believe this was OK. She didn't know her worth. If I accepted her in this state, I would be no better than any other man. It killed me inside, but I had to humbly decline her invitation.

"I don't think this is such a good idea," I said, gently.

Meadow pushed me away and asked, "What do you mean?"

"I just don't think that it's a good idea. I don't need you to thank me like that. That is not why I'm doing it."

"I know what this is. I'm not as pretty as I used to be. I'm not good enough for you. Well screw you, Joseph!" she yelled. Meadow whirled around and stormed back home. I tried to stop her. I grabbed her by the arm but she pulled away.

"Meadow, I don't need that from you. I want all of you, not just the sex," I tried to explain.

"Yeah, right. Every guy wants sex. All you had to do was say that you weren't interested. Go to hell!" she shouted.

"But Meadow..."

"Don't follow me. Don't you dare follow me! You have changed. You're a jerk!" she screamed. I wanted to follow her, but I needed to let her go. Maybe I embarrassed her. She obviously felt some level of rejection. That wasn't my intent. Quite the contrary, I wanted to make her aware of how special she was.

I planned to catch-up with her tomorrow afternoon. That would give her enough time to cool off.

I woke up to the phone ringing. It was Sarah. "Are we still on for tonight?" she asked.

"Yes," I said, reluctantly.

What if Meadow wanted to hang out tonight? What if she wanted to make up for last night? I already made plans to work on her mother's roof. It would just be natural for me to stay over and spend some time with her. Her insecurities would be exacerbated if I told her I already had plans. And If I canceled our date because Meadow decided to stroll into town...? Sarah would go nuts and never speak to me again. I couldn't worry about this relational chaos.

I said, "We're still on," before hanging up the phone.

I took Duke's truck to Mrs. Kat's house. I typically used it to take him to his appointments. But today, I needed it to transport the pressure washer. I arrived at Mrs. Kat's, expecting to make up with Meadow. But Mrs. Kat was alone.

"I knew it was too good to be true. Part of me isn't even sad... just numb. She left this note for you," Mrs. Kat said, with a lifeless voice.

"Sorry for last night... Heading back to L.A."

Her note crushed me. I hoped she understood where I was coming from. I loved her dearly. And I wasn't going to reduce that to a quick roll in the hay! She was worth so much more than that. Every girl is worth more than that.

Sarah picked me up in front of O'Dell's. She pulled up her father's truck with a small pontoon boat hitched to it. "Get in, Joseph. We're going for a boat ride."

We drove to one of the more popular lakes outside of town. Sarah had me throw some dry wood, a lantern, and a couple of backpacks in the boat. Then, we paddled off.

"Isn't this nice? Aren't you glad you agreed to go?" she asked.

"Yes... everything is great, except the mosquitoes."

Aside from the bugs, the boat ride was peaceful. The sounds were so serene. No cash registers ringing in the next order, customers asking me to add extra hot fudge, or the droning noise of the pressure washer engine. All I heard was our paddles brushing the top of the cool lake water, crickets calling their mates, and bullfrogs singing in perfect harmony. It was nice.

After paddling for 15 minutes, Sarah pointed at a spot on the lakeshore.

"There it is."

It was a beautiful piece of shore. It came with a majestic view, free of charge. The setting was perfect for a couple of good friends. The sky was soft and pitch-black. The stars were so clear and pronounced. It seemed like heaven was right on top of us. Our lantern lit the beach, making it ethereally beautiful. Sarah and I built a fire with the dry wood. Then we caught up, laughing and talking for hours, over hot cocoa and s'mores.

Chapter 16

Local Hero No More

It was another busy summer, 8 months since I had seen Meadow last. I wished she would come home. I played out what I would say to her, over and over again. I needed her to know how much I loved her. She was the girl I was waiting for, without a doubt.

Meadow's homecoming may have been up in the air. But an unwanted blast from the past would be back in our town very soon. I picked our small weekly paper off of my porch. The front page read:

Local Hero Suffers Career Ending Injury.

The article was about Logan Stone. Logan had gone on to be very successful. He made it to the NFL. But the article said he injured his throwing shoulder in a car accident. The paper hinted at the possibility of street racing. The damage his shoulder suffered was permanent.

It was weird seeing those headlines. I despised Logan for everything he had done to me. And was disgusted with what he had done to Meadow. I know Meadow made her own choices, but he was a part of her destruction. However, I had matured as a person, and experience had taught me a few things. Even though Logan had put me through a lot, I wouldn't wish his fate on anyone. There is nothing redeeming about having your dreams stripped away.

A couple of weeks went by after I saw the article. I had to close up the shop for half a day. Duke needed me to chauffeur him to his doctor's appointment. My mother refused to trap herself in the same car as him. For that matter, I'm not sure if she could even drive.

Driving Duke around was always awkward. He was uncomfortable with his independence being stripped away. Some days I wanted to scream, "It's not my fault!" at the top of my lungs. But that wouldn't be right. I had to find grace and patience.

The doctor didn't give us any good news. Duke had suffered another minor stroke a month prior, and his health wasn't improving. His lack of progress frustrated him more than anything. My father was a man who was used to being in control. For the first time, his brawn and will were no match for his condition. We pulled up to the house.

"Do you want me to walk you in and fix you some eggs?" I asked, politely. Duke grunted and slammed the door in my face. He didn't want any company. I learned not to push it. I just wished he would accept the reality of the situation and try to be happier.

I arrived to the shop around noon. My mind was full and my heart was heavy. My thoughts were fixated on the day I left Little PJ in Seattle. Maybe I should have stayed with him. I would be over halfway finished with my schooling. I would be moving forward in life. But instead, here I was, back at O'Dell's.

I focused on more constructive thinking. I was young, but I had enough experience to realize that most battles begin in the mind. I needed to focus on my family, now more than ever. Selfish thinking was going to get me nowhere. I pulled out my father's cumbersome key ring, flipping through what seemed like hundreds of keys. One man should not have this many keys, I thought. They made me feel like a janitor or maintenance man. Ironically, I was a little of both.

Ring... Ring... Ring...

I hadn't been in the shop for more than 2 minutes and the phone was already ringing. Part of me didn't want to answer. I hadn't had time to open up.

I answered, "Thank you for calling O'Dell's. How can I help you?"

"Joseph, I'm going to need you to close down the shop early," my mother said, intensely.

"Is everything OK... Is it Duke?" I asked, concerned.

"I can't stand him. You need to come and take care of him. I don't want to deal with it," she complained.

I lost my patience. My father was extremely difficult after doctors' appointments, and there was probably some validity to her complaints. But that was beside the point.

"Mom, I cannot deal with this right now! I know it's difficult but you need to step up. If this shop isn't running we can't pay the bills."

She hung up on me.

An hour went by before I heard the ringing of the shop bell.

"Hey, Sarah."

"Hey, Joseph. Did you hear about Logan?" she asked, excitedly. Logan was the last thing that I wanted to talk about. But I decided to be cordial about the subject.

"Yes, I did. It's too bad about his arm."

"He'll be back in town this weekend. The church is throwing him a welcome home party. I spoke with his mom a few days ago. She said his spirits are high and he'll probably run their vineyards."

"That's nice," I said, in a sarcastic tone.

"Joseph, I know Logan was a jerk in high school but people change. It sounds like he was really humbled by the accident. You should give him a chance. You might be surprised."

"How can you be so sure? I see his looks haven't lost their affect," I sneered.

"This has nothing to do with his looks. I see his mom all the time. She told me that Logan is an entirely different person," she escalated.

I never went to the party, but Sarah did. And in time, I would see her around town with Logan quite frequently. She would never admit it to my face, but she liked him. Logan had taken two girls from me now. But I wondered why I was irritated. I'm sure that I could have been in a relationship with Sarah if I had chosen. But, I was in love with Meadow. I needed to try to be happy for Sarah. Like I said in high school, Sarah was going to make some guy really happy. I just didn't figure that guy would be Logan.

Chapter 17

The Dream

There is something special about Christmas. I'm not sure if it is the gifts, snow, or the spirit of grace that lined the season. I have always been a fan of Christmas. Frankly, I'm not sure where that came from. My parents never celebrated it. It wasn't that they denounced the season altogether, or walked around saying 'humbug' to everyone they met. They became dormant around the holidays. When everyone else was out spreading cheer, they were locking themselves away (my mother especially).

Running the shop and taking on the lion's share of Duke's needs kept me busy, even during the winter months. I made plans to decorate the shop the day after Thanksgiving. But I never got around to it. There was always an excuse. It could be an emergency at home, Mrs. Kat begging me to keep her company, or my obligations at the shop. But this evening would be different. My decorations would take the town's breath away. Granted, it was the night before Christmas Eve, but better late than never.

The shop had been closed for an hour. I had set up and decorated the Christmas tree. I'd moved to the fake icicles when the phone rang. I really didn't want to pick it up. I had a shop to decorate. After three attempts, I finally gave in.

"Merry Christmas..."

"Joseph, is that you? Is that you?"

"Of course it's me, Mrs. Kat. Merry Christmas."

"Oh Joseph, you have no idea how merry of a Christmas it is!" she exclaimed.

"What do you mean?" I asked.

"Meadow is here. She just got here five minutes ago and she..."

I dropped the phone. I was in shock. I hadn't seen Meadow in three years. She didn't send me, or her mother any indication that she was even alive. I had prayed for her safety every night. But some part of me always expected the worst. I wouldn't be decorating tonight, and for good reason. I picked up the phone again.

"Joseph... Joseph... are you there?"

"I'm here. I'm sorry. I dropped the phone. I'm on my way, Mrs. Kat."

The snow fell as I locked the shop doors. It felt like I was in a movie. The whole experience was surreal. The gentle flakes fell on my eyelashes and melted down my cheeks. Maybe I was mistaking melted snow for my tears. This was what Christmas was all about, the gifts you can't buy.

My mind was on autopilot as I drove to Meadow's house. I still can't remember how I got there. I was too busy thinking about what I was going to say. I would not lose her this time. I would win her at any cost. I arrived to her house and I noticed the weirdest sight. Mrs. Kat was sitting on a folding chair on her porch. What could she be doing? It was freezing out there.

"Mrs. Kat, what are you doing out here? Why aren't you inside with Meadow?"

"I was waiting for you, Joseph. She is already talking about leaving in a couple of days. I guess she was just traveling with a boyfriend of hers... or whatever you want to call him. He had some business to take care of in the area. Then they're heading back to California."

Mrs. Kat was wrapped in a blanket and held a tall glass of whiskey. She took a large gulp of the hard stuff. She pleaded, "Joseph, you have to save her. I have a bad feeling. If we don't get her back this time, I just might lose my daughter for good."

I sat on the porch next to Mrs. Kat. I didn't know how to make her feel better. So I decided to be as transparent as possible.

"Mrs. Kat, I love your daughter more than you'll ever know. And I love you so much that it hurts. I want to marry Meadow one day. I want to buy a big house and start a family with her. And you're welcome to come."

"You would let me stay with you two?" she asked, surprised.

"Mrs. Kat, I would take care of you for the rest of your life. But, in the end, our future is Meadow's choice. I've made peace with that. I just hope you have, too."

I walked into the house. Mrs. Kat shuffled past me, went into her room, and shut the door. Meadow was sitting on the couch.

"Merry Christmas, JoJo," she said, with a bowed head.

"Merry Christmas, Meadow."

I took off my coat and hat and placed them on the rack next to the door. Something was wrong. Meadow continued to avoid my gaze. I walked over to the couch, but she clearly didn't want me near her.

"Please don't come any closer. I thought I could face you, but I'm feeling a little weird," she confessed.

"Why would you feel weird?" I asked.

"Just go over to the table. I got you a gift."

I lifted the lid, and discovered ice skates.

"Thank you, Meadow, but you know I don't know how to skate."

"I thought I'd teach you someday," she said, softly.

"I'm awkward. I'm not sure there is enough time in the world," I joked.

"We could go to that lake you took me to a few years ago." She paused, and seemed to make some sort of internal decision. "We can get started tonight, if you want," she offered.

"You want to go to Lonely Lake this late?" I asked, surprised.

"Why not?"

"You're right, why not?"

Taking a deep breath, Meadow stood up and prepared to leave. I got my first good look at her. I realized why Mrs. Kat was worried and, why Meadow felt so insecure. She was wearing an oversized sweatshirt, but it still couldn't hide how much weight she had lost. She must have dropped another twenty pounds. Her hair was lifeless and thinning towards the front, where her bangs used to be. Meadow's eyes were surrounded by dark, lifeless circles. She had sores on her skin and her face was pale. She looked like she had barely made it out of hell. I should have been sad. But my sadness was overpowered by a joy that came from somewhere deep inside. I was just happy that she was here. I looked at her and smiled.

I slowly walked within a few inches of her face. Then, I hugged her. She was so skinny that I could feel her ribcage against my chest. I felt her heartbeat as she exhaled in my embrace. I closed my eyes and got lost in the moment.

"Are you ready to learn how to skate?" she asked, excitedly.

"I'm up for the challenge. Let's head to the lake."

The frozen lake was gorgeous at night. The snow and ice reflected the light of the moon and gave us more ambiance than I'd expected. Meadow still had that spark inside her. She got on the ice and per-formed like she had years ago. To say that I was intimidated was an understatement. After building up enough courage and growing tired of Meadow's joking taunts, I shakily made my way onto the ice. Meadow laughed as I struggled to balance on the skates.

"JoJo, you're a natural," she teased.

"Get over here and help me before I kill myself," I panicked. She grabbed my hands, acting as a support as I bumbled over the ice. I was too busy staring at her to learn a new skill.

"Why are you looking at me like that?" she asked.

"No reason."

"Don't give me that. You've been looking at me like that all night," she snapped.

Meadow quickly skated to shore. I tried my best to keep up, but I didn't have a chance. By the time I made it, she had already changed into her shoes. I hurried and changed into my boots.

"Let's just go," she said, tensing up again.

"What did I do?" I asked, confused.

"You didn't do anything. I just want to go home."

"Meadow, I don't mind taking you home. But the least you can do is tell me what I did. I just don't get it. Help me understand," I pleaded.

She cried, "I have a question for you, JoJo."

"OK... fire away. Ask as many questions as you want."

"How do you look at me like I'm the same girl who walked through the doors of your grandfather's ice-cream shop so long ago? I'm not that girl, and I'm not worth waiting on. So what's your problem? Is this a joke or some sort of game?"

"No, it's not a game," I said, sincerely.

"Then why look at me like that? Can't you see how dirty and disgusting I am? You have no clue of the things I've done... no clue!" she screamed, aggressively pulling at her clothes.

"It doesn't matter," I said, softly.

"What do you mean it doesn't matter? I've tried every drug, slept with more guys than I can remember. Joseph, I've sold my body just to have a place to get a fix."

"It doesn't matter to me, Meadow."

"Are you deaf? I'm a dirty, junkie, whore. I am the lowest. I belong on the streets. Why does that not matter to you? HOW CAN THAT NOT MATTER TO YOU?" she yelled.

"Because God chose you for me!" I shouted back.

"Really... really, Joseph? You think God chose THIS for you?" Meadow rolled up her right sleeve. She exposed the scars and bruises on her arms from the heroin needles.

I gently rolled down her sleeves. I pulled her in close and said, "I told a lie in the shop awhile back. Someone asked me if I loved you, and I said no to save face. I lied, and guess what, Meadow? Grace covers that, too."

"Joseph, there's a big difference between telling a white lie and selling your soul," she argued.

"I see your potential, and I'm not giving up on you. I will never give up on you." We stood there for a couple of uncomfortable moments. I said, "Don't cry, pretty girl."

"Don't call me that. Stop lying to me. Just level with me. Why have you waited on me for so long? I never told you I wanted to be with you. And a girl like me isn't even worth your time. I've been around a lot of men, Joseph. And none of them have come close to treating me like you do. So why? Why are you waiting on me?"

She forced my hand. I had held back the reason for so long. If I didn't tell her tonight, I would lose her for good.

"I will tell you. But you have to promise not to freak out."

"I won't freak out," she said confidently.

"No... you don't understand. Promise me again," I said, sternly.

"I won't. I promise," she said, softly.

"A year before you came into town, I had a dream. I saw a girl with blondish-brown hair, hazel-green eyes, and an olive complexion. It was you. I saw you before you came here. I heard a voice. It was as clear as yours and mine. Maybe it was my subconscious, maybe it was an angel, maybe it was the voice of God Himself. All I know for sure is that the voice gave me crystal clear directions. It said: *It will be the toughest thing you ever do. But tell the girl to have faith and wait on her. She will restore something in your life that you cannot restore on your own.* I know that girl is you. I saw you in my dreams. I don't care what you've done or who you've been with. I don't care how many mistakes you've made. You're a gift, whether you know it or not. I love you, and I will be here when your life turns around. Have faith... I will wait on you."

I had finally told her. It was like a weight being lifted off my shoulders. I just hoped she took my confession into consideration. I didn't want her to leave. I was staring into the eyes of my wife. And I was ready to be her husband.

Meadow stopped crying and gave me a smile. There was hope in her smile. Then, she placed her frail, bony hand in mine. She still wore the bracelet. It didn't have the luster it'd once had. But the promise was still there.

"Take me home, JoJo," she asked, humbly.

I said my peace before Meadow went inside. "I love you more than you'll ever know. I want to start a life with you, Meadow. I just don't..."

She cut me off and said, "Joseph, you've already said a lot tonight."

"I thought you weren't going to freak out," I said.

"I'm not. I need time to digest it. Come back tomorrow. We can go out for lunch."

"I'd like that," I said, smiling.

The next day, I drove to Meadow's. I couldn't wait to take her out to lunch. My spirits were high until I parked. Something was wrong.

I could feel a certain heaviness. Mrs. Kat's door was ajar. Normally, this wouldn't have caused me any concern, but my senses were heightened. I walked through the cracked door. The house was in shambles. The kitchen table was turned over, clutter was strewn about the living room, and pictures hung on the wall askew. There were all the signs of a struggle.

Mrs. Kat was sitting on her couch, a half-gallon bottle of whiskey in her hands. Most of the contents were consumed. She put the bottle to her lips and took two, huge gulps. She was going to kill herself. I stumbled over the mess and sat next to her. I tried to gently remove the bottle from her hands. But she pulled it back into her possession.

"She was a girl who lied a lot," Mrs. Kat slurred. I didn't know where she was going with this. But I sat quietly and listened. "Meadow lied a lot. She lied about stealing out of my purse. She lied about skipping school. She lied about her grades. But she wasn't lying about her father molesting her. Her father molested her for six years, underneath my nose."

My heart sank. It all made sense... so much sense. It took everything inside of me not to ball up and cry like a baby. But she wasn't done.

"He is a really prominent banker in Seattle. We lived in a beautiful house. I thought I had it all, Joseph. I had the stuff that all little girls dream of. I had the white picket fence, the handsome husband who had diligently worked his way up the company ladder, and a beautiful baby girl.

"There was a time when we gave her the best. We put her in ice-skating and ballet. We enrolled her into private school. She had phenomenal grades. But all hell broke loose around the time she turned eight. Meadow started having trouble at school. She was eventually kicked out for her behavior.

"Meadow was an absolute terror at home. She disrespected me constantly and called me every name in the book. I looked to her dad for help, but he was too busy with work. It was like the perfect storm.

He worked long days, and wanted nothing to do with me, at night. I thought he was having an affair. He had a young secretary. Her dresses always hugged her in all the right places.

"A year went by and nothing changed. Meadow's behavior got worse, and her dad was hardly ever around. And even when he was, he was distant. That's when I turned to the bottle. Alcohol was the only thing that made me feel better. I drank until I passed out every night. I did this for years.

"But one night, it was different. I drank as I did every day. I drank so much that I passed out... more like blacked out. Honestly, I was trying to kill myself. I drank a fifth of whiskey and added some pills to the cocktail. I was knocked out cold when I heard a voice in the darkness. '*Get up. Get up, Katherine. Get up, something isn't right.*' I stumbled to my feet, and crawled up the stairs to check on Meadow.

"There the bastard was! He was in my daughter's room, raping her. It took everything inside of me not to faint. My knees began to buckle. I used the doorframe to hold myself up. He noticed me stammering in the door. But he didn't stop Joseph... He didn't even stop... he said, 'Leave, and close the door behind you'. I grabbed Meadow's lamp and I hit him over the head with it. I didn't have my balance, so I fell. He was furious. He got up and punched me in the face, over and over again. Then, he grabbed me by the hair, pulled me to my feet, and threw me down the stairs.

"I woke up in the hospital. I was in a coma for a few days. He told the nurses that I was an alcoholic. And that I stumbled out of the house and got mugged. Of course, everyone believed him. He was connected. He was untouchable.

"After I recovered, I told him that I was going to the police. He said that they would never believe a drunk like me. He settled for divorcing me. He bought this rundown shack for us. He wanted us to be as far from him as possible. He barely gives me enough money every month to survive. I blow most of it on liquor.

"I thought that this town might turn things around for Meadow. But it hasn't, things got worse. My worst nightmares have come true," she cried.

"I'm so sorry, Mrs. Kat. I am so very sorry," I said, through teary eyes.

Something came alive in Mrs. Kat, like she had snapped out of a trance. "Oh God... what did I just say? Joseph, please don't mind me. It's just the alcohol talking," she said, nervously.

"Ok, it's just the alcohol," I agreed, even though I knew it wasn't the alcohol. She had, indeed, told me the truth. But I didn't want to push the subject, and make her uncomfortable. "Where's Meadow?" I asked.

"Her boyfriend came back this morning. I begged her to stay. I told her how sorry I was... how much I loved her. But none of it worked. She insisted on leaving. So I locked the door and stood in front of it. She fought me to get out of this house."

"I'm sure she'll come back. She always does," I said, confidently. I tried to keep my responses short. I didn't want to elaborate too much. My heart hurt over what they had been through. And now was not the time to be emotional. I needed to get the whiskey away from Mrs. Kat before she hurt herself.

"Joseph, you are my last hope. I don't pray. If there is a God, how could He let this happen? But, I do believe in fate. We met you for a reason. You will help make up for my mistakes. I still believe that your love can bring her back home for good. Do you believe that, Joseph?" she asked, expectantly.

"I do. You need to eat something, Mrs. Kat. Why don't you lie down while I fix something?"

"OK. You know best," she said, passively.

I scoured her cupboards. All she had was some dry oatmeal. Mrs. Kat passed out before I could bring the water to a boil. I pulled a blanket over her. I finished preparing the meal and straightened up the house. I poured the rest of her whiskey out and left a note that read, "Please eat," on the coffee table.

I drove to the grocery store and bought enough food to fill her refrigerator and pantry. She was still passed out when I returned. I looked at her with a new respect. She had been through so much and she hadn't given up. Mrs. Kat was a fighter. I'm not sure why she recanted her confession. Maybe she thought it was going to scare me off, or maybe she was overcome by shame. Either way, I understood. Their story didn't make me think any less of them. If anything, it made me love them that much more.

"I can't do this. I just can't!" Bridgett Marie shouted, before standing up.

"What's wrong?" I asked.

"What's wrong? Don't you have something for me to actually DO around here? I'm a caretaker, not a counselor."

I began coughing violently. I pulled my hands from my mouth. Blood soiled my palms.

"Mr. Joseph!!!" she screamed.

"Please get me a tissue. The medicine is wearing off," I said, shaking. I cleared my throat and spit the rest of the blood into a Kleenex. I threw the gob into the trashcan next to my bed.

"I need to call a doctor," she said, frantically.

"No... you can't. Whatever you do, don't call a doctor!" I yelled.

Bridgett Marie said, "But, Mr. Joseph, I have to do something. It's my job."

I rebutted, "Your job is to take care of me. And the only way to do that, is by listening to this story."

She sat back in the chair. Shaking her head, she said, "You don't even know me. You're trusting me with something so precious, and it makes me feel like crap."

"Why does it upset you?" I asked, confused.

"Because, I'm not who you think I am. If you knew what I was planning to do this morning, you wouldn't even let me change your bedpan."

"What do you mean child? Please talk to me," I pleaded. Her right hand shook uncontrollably. Tears welled up in her eyes. I grabbed her hand in an attempt to comfort her.

She said, softly, "Do you remember how my phone kept ringing this morning?"

"Yes, I do, honey. Whoever was calling seemed to upset you."

She continued, "His name is Tyson. A friend of mine snuck me into a club. She knew the bouncers. So, I didn't have to show my I.D. I was dancing when I felt an unfamiliar hand on my hip. Before I could turn around, a voice as smooth as silk asked, 'Do you want to dance?' He was quite a bit older than me. But I didn't mind. He smelled so good. He didn't carry himself like guys my age. It felt new and nice. He bought me a few drinks. I knew I shouldn't have let him, but I didn't want to seem young and scared. We ended up at a hotel that night and... you know. I went home the next morning feeling so ashamed. I called him a few times, but he never answered. A couple of weeks went by. I was walking in the mall. I saw Tyson walking out of Macy's. I contemplated confronting him. I wanted to know why he used me. Out of nowhere, two kids ran out of the department store and grabbed his legs. They were followed by his wife. They kissed there, rings on and everything. I walked towards him. When he saw me, his eyes went lifeless. But I let it be. I got really sick. I was throwing up every morning. I... I..."

She sobbed uncontrollably. Then, she placed my hand or her stom-ach. There was life inside of her. She was pregnant with Tyson's child.

She cried, "I left him a message that got his attention. I said, 'I know you're married, but you don't know that I'm pregnant.' He tried to convince me that an abortion was best for the both of us. But I wasn't so sure. I didn't want anything from him... but I didn't feel right just getting rid of... If I waited any longer, I wouldn't be able to... to... I can't even say it. We were scheduled to get the procedure done this morning. I was making my way there when the agency called. They asked if I could fill in for Felicia. That's why he kept calling this morn-ing. He knew it was our last chance to get rid of my baby. Mr. Joseph, I'm not the best person. You need to know this before you share any more with me." She buried her head in her hands and wept. I took some tissue, and wiped the tears from her pretty cheekbones.

In a soft voice, I said, "If you look at the vast sea of humanity, you won't find Satan or Jesus. We all lie somewhere in-between. No one should be defined by a momentary lapse in judgment, no matter how big or small. Forgiveness is releasing all hope for a better past. Forgive *yourself, Bridgett Marie. We are as good as our next decision. You being here is no accident. I need you to help me close the most important chapter of my life. Please help me. Please listen to this story."*

"I'll listen, Mr. Joseph," she said, in a redeemed tone.

Chapter 18

It Couldn't Be

Two years had passed since Meadow left. Two years without any communication – not even a postcard. Still, Mrs. Kat and I both had a tremendous faith that she would return. But we didn't dwell on it.

Mrs. Kat was in a good place. We had grown closer than ever. I upped my visits to twice a week. In a weird way, she became a mother to me. She was still a bit dysfunctional, but who was I to talk. At least she was there for me, unlike Gloria.

We took on domestic projects together. One week, we'd plant some rosebushes along her property. The next week, we'd remodel a small area of her house.

I had to believe that confessing her ex-husband's heinous actions was medicine for Mrs. Kat's soul. And even though she'd recanted her statements, she knew I was smart enough to know better. All in all, I was so proud of her.

Mrs. Kat cut down on her bad habits and picked up some better ones. She reduced her drinking. She had a nightcap (every night). But she didn't drink as much during the day. I couldn't wait for the day she'd give it up cold turkey. But even so, less alcohol meant more production. Most days, she cleaned the house spotless. This freed up time for different things.

Mrs. Kat was an avid fisher, but she hadn't done it in years. I introduced her to some of the lakes outside of town. She never came home empty-handed. She even worked at the shop once a week. I grossly overpaid her, but I didn't mind. She was my mother-in-law to be. I was set on taking care of her for the rest of my life. But those plans would come to an earth-shattering halt.

There are some days that are etched in your memory forever. This day was more than that. It was like someone shoved a fiery-hot cattle brand into the flesh of my brain. I remember what I wore and that I regretted not shaving before coming to work that morning. I even remember that the shop was low on strawberry ice cream, just before that terrible call.

"O'Dell's Creamery, this is…"

"I know who this is!" she screamed.

"Mrs. Kat?"

"Don't you say my name. Don't you ever say my name again. I HATE YOU, JOSEPH!"

"Mrs. Kat, calm down. What is this about?"

"You were supposed to save her. Meadow killed herself last night."

Click.

I couldn't believe my ears. My brain refused to process her words. I grabbed my clunky keys and sprinted for Duke's truck. I didn't even lock up. I had to get to Mrs. Kat as fast as possible. It had to be some sort of misunderstanding. I bolted up her stairs and pounded on her door.

Bang, bang, bang.

"Open up, Mrs. Kat! Open up! Come on, Mrs. Kat, please open up!" I shouted, frantically.

Mrs. Kat opened her side window and heaved junk in my direction. She slung glasses that shattered at my feet. Then she grabbed a bottle of whiskey and threw it at my head. There was broken glass everywhere.

"Get off my porch!" she screamed, as she fetched more ammunition. I got off of her porch but I didn't leave her property.

"What happened, Mrs. Kat?"

"She died of an overdose. She killed herself. You were supposed to save her but you didn't. I never want to see you again," she sobbed.

"But, Mrs. Kat…"

"Don't you *but* me. You were supposed to bring back my baby, but you failed, Joseph. YOU failed! If you come by here again, I swear I will get a restraining order or call the police. And if that doesn't work, I will shoot you myself." Mrs. Kat slammed the window, almost breaking the glass set in its frame.

I don't remember driving back to the shop. Part of my brain shut off. Maybe it was a survival mechanism to help me cope. There were a few people sitting in the booths and a couple of people standing in line. They must have thought that I was in the back, and would be out shortly. The site was so unsettling. I had just lost her, and already people were asking me to serve them.

"Get out. Everyone get out! She's dead! She's dead!! Get out!!!" I shouted. I scared the life out of every, last customer. They ran for the exit and I locked the door behind them. My knees gave out. I was unable to walk.

I crawled across the red-and-white-checkered floor until I reached the inventory room. It was there that I broke down. I remember thinking to myself, 'Meadow was right. There is no God.' The proof was overwhelming. My dream was nothing more than a coincidence.

Meadow committed suicide and Mrs. Kat wanted nothing more to do with me. Little PJ was off finishing his degree. Sarah was head-over-heels for Logan Stone. Duke was a fraction of the man he used to be. And my clinically depressed mother didn't have the capacity to acknowledge my existence.

All I had left was the shop, and that cursed town. I was destined to be a nobody. I was nothing more than a fixture in that tourist trap. I was a man without a dream. I was worthless.

I pounded my fist against the cold floor and cried out. I screamed profanities and kicked holes in the walls. I punched the tile, until it removed the flesh from my knuckles. The tile, the grout, all of it was stained red with my blood.

I carried on like this for hours. Something died inside of me and I fought to get it back. But it, like Meadow, was dead and gone. Faith gone, I wept and wailed until I passed out from exhaustion.

I awoke to the sound of the phone ringing. It was dark outside. I had been out for hours. I thought to myself, 'Maybe it was just a bad dream.' But I saw the dry blood and knew it was true.

"Hello..." I said, weakly.

"Joseph, your father won't eat. He's so prideful. Why does he put me through this? I can't do this anymore."

I took a tone with my mother that I had never taken before. "You can't do this anymore? NO... I CAN'T DO THIS ANYMORE!!! I just lost the most important person in my entire life. She's dead, D.E.A.D. dead! You married him, so deal with it. Get some real problems and leave me the hell alone!" I screamed.

I slammed the phone down five or six times, before finally hanging up. I stood with my elbows on the counter and my face buried deep in my hands. I heard someone trying to open the front door. They tapped on the glass. I thought they would give up, but they didn't. They started banging on the glass. I looked up to see who it was. It was Sarah.

"GO AWAY!" I shouted.

But Sarah shook her head "no", and continued tapping on the glass. I could hear her muffled voice.

"Open the door, Joseph." She wouldn't give up. She stood there for at least ten minutes. I finally gave in. She tried hugging me, but I pushed her away.

"Save it for your boyfriend," I sneered.

Logan was waiting in his car outside. They had become really close. The two had been dating, officially, for the past couple of months. I still resented their relationship.

"Joseph, why are you pushing me away? I came as soon as I heard."

"I guess news travels fast in this town."

"Are you OK?"

"Does it look like I'm OK? DOES IT?"

"Your hands are bleeding! What have you done to yourself?" she cried, before grabbing at my hands.

I pulled away and yelled, "Don't touch me!"

"Joseph, please don't yell at me," she cried.

I was going to hurt her feelings and I didn't care. For the first time, I didn't care about anyone else but myself.

"Get out of here. I don't want to see your face again. You never liked her anyway. You were jealous of her. You're probably glad she's dead. You're happy aren't you? Get out and go run to your boyfriend and go have your perfect, little life."

Sarah slapped me across the face. Then she pushed me repeatedly before saying, "Joseph, I've always loved you. How could you treat me like this?"

"It's simple. I never loved you," I said, cruelly.

Sarah gasped. And, with tear-filled eyes, she left the creamery.

I walked aimlessly around the town that night. It was a place for the washed-up. I wasn't going to run away from this abyss anymore, not even in my imagination. I would embrace it. I fell short, like everyone else who lived there.

Eventually, I found myself on the shores of Lonely Lake. I could hear the life along the water, creatures both big and small existing together. And somehow it just worked for them.

The water was still and peaceful. I wondered how the tapestry of life could abide so effortlessly. But man, God's greatest creation, couldn't. The order on the lake worked, but there was no order in life. There was no reward for being a good person, just pain. Maybe Logan was right. There are only two types of people: those who use others, and those who are used.

The night was clear and pitch-black. For the first time, I was not enchanted by the stars. The sky was nothing more than a black abyss, disrupted by speckles of light... nothing more, nothing less. I was surrounded by nothingness.

I addressed the heavens in a belligerent tone: *The idea that some-one or something is watching out for us, is a crock of shit. Did you know that he started raping her at age eight? Her own father! She lived through that hell, over and over again. She probably called out for her mama. But mama didn't answer. She was drunk and passed out in the next room. How many times did that little girl cry out before she realized help would never come? Did you hear her voice? Did you even care? You should have killed her then!!! Oh that's right. You couldn't have helped, because you don't exist. It's just us. Life is nothing more than a bunch of selfish people, destroying each other. Meadow was right.*

My heart was pierced, and my soul seeped out, until there was nothing left. I had changed. For once in my life, I was going to be in control. No one else.

When I got home, there was a note on the kitchen table. Little PJ had called me three times. Sarah must have called him.

"Hello."

"It's Joseph," I said, wearily.

"Joseph, I'm on my way right now. Don't worry. Just give me a couple of days to get my stuff together..."

"No you're not." I interrupted

"What do you mean?"

"This place is cursed."

"But you need me and I'm your friend," he pleaded.

"Little PJ, if you come back here, I swear on Meadow's grave, I will never talk to you again."

"But Joseph..."

Click.

I decided that night that everything would change, starting with the creamery.

———&—————

"What? What do you mean, she killed herself? That's not possible," Bridgett Marie gasped.

"It's true... she took her life."

My coughing fits came back. I tried my best to keep the blood down. "Bridgett Marie, can you get me some water?"

She grabbed my coffee cup and returned with cold tap water. "Thank you," I said.

"Mr. Joseph, you don't look so good." She pressed the back of her hand against my head. She said, "You're burning up. I need to get a thermometer!"

"It doesn't matter," I snapped.

"This is crazy," she snapped back.

I pleaded, "Please, sit down and listen. The story has to end this way."

"OK, Mr. Joseph," she said hesitantly.

My body was dripping with sweat. And it was getting tougher to breathe. It was almost time to go. But I would not leave until my work was done.

Chapter 19

O'Dell's Diner?

There are certain experiences that break the heart for good. Nothing short of a miracle can heal it. The miracle always comes, but most are too jaded to recognize it. I was numb to the touch, like a dead man walking. I had no purpose, and I had given up.

I had grown to dislike people. I tried to get away from those I grew up with. I didn't want to face them, or their handouts. Their words couldn't comfort me.

I turned O'Dell's creamery into a run of the mill diner. It was open 24 hours a day, 7 days a week. I advertised on the interstate. This brought a lot of truckers, wanderers, and lost souls into the shop, especially on my shift. I worked graveyard, from 8:00pm 'till 6:00am. I gave the day shift to Little PJ's eldest brother and his wife. They were hard workers and were happy to escape the fields.

It wasn't a good business decision. The nightshift sales did not make up for the wages I paid out. But the change bought me some peace. I just wanted to mingle with strangers. My lonely routine was interrupted at least once a month. Burm, Mrs. Pittman, Jimmy, Sarah, Pastor Paul, and Papa Pete all took turns trying to save me. But there's no use throwing a life-ring to someone who's determined to drown.

They tried every trick in the book to reach out to me. One night, around 3:00am, Jimmy came in the shop. The locals never came in that late, even the ones that wanted to help.

"What will it be?" I asked, coldly.

"I'll have the soup. I'm having a little trouble sleeping."

I scooped up some soup and placed it in front of Jimmy. I would not be goaded into small talk. Jimmy spooned the lukewarm broth into his mouth. He said, "I see you're still wearing the bracelet."

I hated that he noticed it on my wrist. I didn't have the courage to take it off. It was all I had left of her.

He muttered, "You know, your grandfather..."

I interrupted, "Don't bring him into this. I don't want to hear any of your stupid stories. I don't need your sympathy. You have two choices; eat your soup quietly or get out of my shop."

Jimmy slapped the bowl of soup off the counter and stood up. "Who do you think you're talking to?" he yelled.

"I'm talking to you, old fool," I jabbed back.

Our eyes met for a moment. I thought we were going to tussle in the shop. But Jimmy's bottom lip quivered. He pointed, six inches from my face, and said, "You're a coward. You're just like everyone else around here. When I gave you those bracelets, I trusted you with my most precious possessions. But you fooled me, Joseph."

I interjected, "What do you mean, I fooled you?"

"Just shut up and listen!" he bellowed. Jimmy paced the floor and rubbed the back of his neck before speaking again. "I told you to love without reservation. That includes death. Love is the only force strong enough to conquer the grave. We honor the lost by thriving, especially in their absence. Love, in its purest form, is an action. And you're only as good as your next decision. I know you're hurting, Joseph. But, if you're going to throw away all you've done up to this point... if you're going to piss on the greatest example of love this town has ever seen... if you're going to shame Meadow's memory, then do me a favor... Bury that bracelet in the ground, too."

He stormed out of the shop before I could respond. It was better that way. I would have said something I'd have regretted.

I changed a lot of things at home. I spent more time taking care of Duke. I didn't want to hear my mother's incessant complaining. Despite myself, I formed a quiet respect for my father. His dream of playing football was as real to him as my dream of being with Meadow. When his dream came crashing down, he swallowed his pride and worked at the shop. He worked his butt off for an ungrateful wife and naive kid. I finally understood the source of Duke's anger. I wished I could go back, before his stroke, and apologize. He was right all along. Why did I focus on the silly things?

I was working on a Wednesday night... I guess it was Thursday morning. It was around 2:00am. The most unexpected guest walked in. It was Sarah. She came to the shop at least once a week after Meadow's death. I never talked about Meadow and she never spoke of Logan. We made small talk, ignoring the heavier things. It was her own, little way of making sure I was OK. And, even though I never expressed it, it meant the world to me. However, her visiting me this late was strange.

"What are you doing here so late?" I asked.

"Joseph, I don't want you to say anything. I just need you to listen. Please listen carefully."

"OK..."

"Logan asked me to marry him," she explained.

"Congrats," I said, in a very condescending tone.

"Really, Joseph?" she said, in a hurt tone. Tears streamed down her face. She officially had my attention. "He asked me to marry him, and it would be a good fit. His family alone could make sure that my father's church never had another worry. And I would feel totally secure. But there's a problem, Joseph. I have this huge monkey on my back, because every moment I spend with him, I wish it was with you. He has changed. He's a really decent man. But he isn't you. I've tried loving him. I've tried really hard, but I can't get you out of my head and heart. I want to be with you. So give me the word, and I won't accept his proposal. I will spend the rest of my life with you," she said, tenderly.

"I'm damaged goods, Sarah. Trust me, you're better off with Logan."

"I know you're hurting, but I will be there for you. I'll stick by your side no matter how long it takes. You'll find your old self again. You just need time, and someone who cares," she said.

"Isn't that the problem with people? We are always trying to fix each other. We always want what we can't have. I chased after love once, and what did it get me? Nothing. It was a waste of time. Take my advice. Go marry him. Stop following your heart and listen to your head. Don't make the same mistake I did."

"Joseph... this isn't about you and Meadow. This is about you and me. It can be different."

"Would you like to hear about our specials? We have excellent burgers and fries."

"Dammit, Joseph, she's dead!!!" she screamed.

"You don't think I know that?" I yelled.

"You may know that, but you're failing to realize I'm here. While you still live with the idea of Meadow, I'm here, and I'm yours if you want."

"Sarah..."

"Yes, Joseph?"

"I think you should start shopping for wedding dresses. Logan is a lucky man," I said, coldly.

The annoying shop bell rang as she ran out of the shop, crying. I felt bad for what I said. I loved Sarah. She was one of my best friends. But I gave her the right advice. She needed to do the smart thing.

It was approaching the slowest part of the night. I decided to go to the back and do some inventory. When I returned, I was startled by a man sitting quietly at one of the barstools. It was unusual. I always heard the bell ring, even when I was in the back.

I could tell the guy wasn't from around these parts. He was dressed like a trucker. His skin was a light-brown complexion and his hair was dark and wavy. He looked like he was from some tropical island.

"Hello." I can't explain it, but something about the way he said hello brought me a familiar comfort.

"How can I help you?" I asked.

"I would really like some coffee."

"No problem... coming right up. I haven't seen you around here before. What's your name, stranger?"

"My name is Pana... Pana Mamea."

"What kind of name is that? Oh, I'm sorry. I didn't mean to be rude," I said, embarrassed.

"It's fine. I get it a lot. It's Samoan."

"What brings you here, Pana?"

He didn't answer me right away. He just smiled. His smile warmed my dormant heart. I felt better than I had in a long time.

"I'm a long-haul trucker. I drove up from California and made a delivery in Seattle. I have one last stop, in Spokane, before heading back home. I saw your sign on the interstate and figured I'd stop in. You never told me your name, young man."

"It's Joseph."

"Ah, Joseph... that is a good name. There have been a lot of Joseph's who have done great things throughout time. Your parents made a good choice."

"I'll make sure to tell them that," I said, jokingly.

I poured Pana a cup of coffee. He reached for the creamer. I couldn't help but notice his hands. They were too nice to be trucker hands.

"Joseph, you are out of creamer. Do you mind getting me some?"

I could have sworn I filled up the containers before my shift. I went back and grabbed some more. When I returned, Pana was gone.

My mind tried, confusedly, to process what happened. I hadn't heard a big truck pull up in front of the shop. And furthermore, I didn't hear the shop bell when Pana entered or left. I opened the door to make sure the bell still worked. It rang like usual. He left enough money to pay for the coffee three times over. Under the money was a napkin with writing on it. It said: *The key is with you.*

The entire experience shook me to the bone. Then the eeriest feeling came over me. I was the only one in the shop, but I didn't feel alone. What did the note mean? I called Little PJ's brother at 5:00am. I told him that the shop would be closed until Monday for renovations. I needed to close it down for a few days and collect myself. I could not shake this feeling. Something was happening inside of me.

It was around 7:00am. I checked on my father before going to bed. The note on the napkin bothered me. What key did I have? I tossed and turned for an hour. I couldn't sleep, so I got up and fixed Duke some breakfast. I asked him, over and over again, if he needed anything else. He gestured that he was fine. His speech wasn't the greatest. When he spoke, I was reminded of his impairment. I went back to bed around noon, and fell fast asleep.

I opened my eyes. My clock read 7:37pm. I assumed it was all a dream. I reached in my pocket for my keys. I felt the napkin. I read the message over and over again. I asked myself, "What key? What does it mean?" I plopped on my bed in aggravation. A sharp pain shot up my leg. I had sat on my father's key chain. I chucked the keys out of frustration. They landed on my grandfather's desk.

I decided to go to work. I wasn't going to be moved by this foolishness. I went to retrieve the keys from the desk. I gasped, "It couldn't be..."

I had been carrying my father's keys since his first stroke. They were the keys to the truck, the shop, and our house. I hadn't noticed it before, but a small key lay hidden on the key ring. The way the ring landed on my grandfather's desk showcased the key. But, could he have had *that* key all along? How could I have missed it? I inserted it in the keyhole that locked the mysterious top drawer of the desk. The key fit like a hot knife through butter. I slowly opened the drawer.

Oh my God. I stared at the contents, almost uncomprehending. I called out loudly to my mother. "GLORIA... GLORIA... *GLORIA!!!*"

She ran down the steps.

"Explain this!"

Chapter 20

The Explanation

Some memories are locked away for years, for decades, even. And some family secrets are never meant to be exposed. I wasn't quite sure what I was looking at, but I knew it had to be explained. The drawer was filled with old family pictures. One picture caught my attention, in particular.

It was taken in front of the creamery. Duke, my mother, and my grandfather were in it. But that wasn't the puzzling part. The picture also showed my grandfather holding a little boy, who looked just like me... it had to be me. I was around two or three years old. Duke had his arm around my mother and she was pregnant. How could she be pregnant? I was an only child. And, if she was pregnant with me, who was my grandfather holding?

I noticed shears in my mother's hand. She was on her way to trim the bushes. I asked my mother to explain the picture. She looked like she had seen a ghost. I grew tired of her standing there, dumbfounded, as I questioned her.

"Mother, explain what this is all about. Please tell me what's going on," I pleaded.

"I don't have to explain anything to you. Why don't you mind your own business and stay in your place?" she said, bitterly. Gloria headed for the stairs. I bounded in front of her.

"What are you going to do, hold me prisoner? Let me through," she said, nervously. My mother tried to push through me, but I didn't let her. She wailed on my chest with her free hand. "Get out of the way! Get out of my way, Joseph!" she screamed.

I did something I had never done before. I embraced my mother, and I didn't let her go. She fought hard, but I held her without recess.

With all the strength I could muster, I said, "Mom its OK. Whatever secret you and Duke kept from me... I get it. You've been holding on to something so heavy that you just shut down. You go numb, so the pain doesn't eat you alive. But it does anyway. I finally get it. But I need you, mom." She continued to fight me, but I refused to let her go.

I felt a hot sensation. It was followed by warmth that coated my arm. The garden tool had cut through the flesh of my forearm. I stumbled back and sat on the staircase. Gloria held the shears with both hands, and pointed the bloody blades in my direction.

Shivering, she screamed, "Move... move out of my way or I'll put these right through you. I swear I will!!!"

Lip quivering, I cried, "You can't kill me, mom. I'm already dead." I buried my face in my hands and wept, "I need you, mom. I still love you, no matter what. It's going to be OK, I promise. Everything is going to be OK. I need you, mom... I need you."

Motherly instincts that had lay dormant, for decades, came alive in Gloria. She sobered from her trance, and threw the shears. She picked up a nearby shirt. My mother gingerly wrapped the white button-up around my wound. She sat next to me and laid her head on my shoulder. We had never shared a tender moment like this. She broke down in my arms, and soaked my shirt with her tears.

"Her name was supposed to be Lilly... Lilly Elizabeth O'Dell," she said.

She walked me over to the couch. I held her hands, trying to provide any comfort I could. I handed her the picture. It had crumpled during our struggle.

"Who's Lilly," I asked.

Overwhelmed with emotion, she said, "That beautiful boy your grandfather is holding is you. We were a happy family, once. Your Grandpa Joe and Duke had a rare closeness. They ran the shop with a joy. Your father was such a goofball around Grandpa Joe. Every other weekend, they'd go fishing together. I couldn't have married into a better family.

"When we got pregnant with you, I felt like the 'first lady'. Both of them waited on me hand and foot. You should have seen your father. He was so proud. You were so spoiled. I practically fought to hold you.

"But, when you were old enough to choose, you always went to your grandfather. He was your favorite. You would climb down those stairs backwards and sit in his lap while he painted. You wouldn't make a peep. It was magic to watch.

"I got pregnant again when you were around two and a half. I had just taken up gardening. There was something about tilling life in the garden while your sister grew inside of me. It brought me so much happiness.

"Tragedy struck us in October, a month before Lilly was due. Your grandfather died from a sudden heart attack. Duke wasn't ready to lose his best friend. He fell into a deep depression. As a matter of fact, you both did. You climbed down those stairs and waited at your grandfather's desk. You weren't old enough to understand that he wasn't coming back. Whenever you'd see his picture or artwork, you'd ask for him. Your father locked every picture of your grandfather in that drawer. And he took his artwork off the walls and put it in boxes. He hated seeing you hurt.

"I went into labor with Lilly in November. Your father was in the shop when I went to the hospital. He rushed there, like a madman, when he found out. But, by the time he arrived, I had already had Lilly, and she didn't survive the delivery.

"I sat there, holding her in my arms. She was the spitting image of your father. I had never cried like that before. I had failed Lilly... I failed Duke."

"Mom, it wasn't your fault. You have to know that."

"It sure felt like it, Joseph. Duke wouldn't come in the room. He just stood in the doorway. I needed him so badly. I needed him to say it wasn't my fault and that he loved me. But he didn't. He just gave me a blank stare, and went back to that damn shop to work. A couple of days went by and I approached Duke about funeral arrangements. He said, *'Funeral arrangements for what?'* Those words forever changed me.

"I buried our daughter by myself. It rained the day of her funeral, and I couldn't have felt more alone. After that day, I didn't love your father anymore. I barely respected him. We basically stayed together for you.

"In the end, I'm not quite sure why I took it out on you. In a strange way, I felt that if I had to let Lilly go; it was only right to let you go, too. I've been no better, to you, than Duke was, to me. And for that, I'm sorry. I'd like to make things better. But, to be honest, I wouldn't know where to start."

The worst pain in the world comes from the unknown. My mother's tears carried over two decades of pain. She grabbed my hands as I wiped them from her cheeks. I finally understood why the garden was her only source of joy. I finally knew why she was so depressed in the winter. I came to understand Duke. He wasn't a monster, just a man, consumed by pain and regret.

Tenderly, I said, "Things could change, you know."

"Do you really think so?" she asked, expectantly.

"Yes, I do. Let's start today," I said, with a smile.

"I'd like that," she said.

"Mom, I know that Duke wasn't there for you when Lilly died. But he hadn't even had time to mourn his father's death. He pushed his family away and embraced strangers. Strangers don't ask you tough questions. They don't remind you of your failure. And they don't require your strength. I get it. I did the same thing when Meadow died. And Duke had it worse. He lost his father and his unborn daughter within a month of each other. I know you needed him, but he really needed you, too. Respectfully, the truth of the matter is, you gave up on each other."

My mother buried her face into my shirt and sobbed. I stroked her hair and brought her in close. "You have nothing to be ashamed of. I'm just glad that you could finally talk about this. I know that things are going to get brighter from here. I'll be here for you, mom. You won't have to do this on your own."

With tear-soaked cheeks, Gloria O'Dell smiled at me for the first time. It almost broke my heart in two. She kissed me on the cheek and gave me a hug.

"Joseph, do you mind if we catch-up?"

"What do you want to know?" I asked, with a smile.

"I want to know everything I've missed. I want to get to know my son."

We talked for hours that night. I let her into my entire life. I told her the adventures little PJ and I had. I introduced her to Meadow and the dream. I recapped junior year and senior prom. I talked about Sarah's love for me, and how I had come to love her, too. We talked about Meadow being sexually abused, her drug overdose, and how Mrs. Kat banished me from her home. Then we cried some more. I told her about Pana Mamea, and I showed her the napkin from the shop. Lastly, I showed her my bracelet. I explained its significance. She gave me a hug and another kiss on the cheek. Being kissed by my mother was like being embraced by God Himself.

It was 5:00am when she made her way to the stairs. "Can we continue to catch-up, Joseph?" she asked.

"Mom... we can catch-up for the rest of our lives," I assured her.

Gloria smiled, and then retreated to her room. I slept with a peace that I had never felt before. I didn't toss or turn. I just rested.

The next few weeks were awkward. My relationship with Gloria was growing at a steady pace. But she and Duke had not found their stride. We did not flaunt our newfound relationship. The last thing we wanted was to alienate Duke, or cause him more pain.

My mother tried being more considerate of his needs. She fetched his morning paper and prepared his coffee. He was grateful, but he didn't see her gestures for what they were; an opportunity to rekindle their relationship. One night, she pulled me to the side and asked for my advice.

"Son, I don't know how to make things right with Duke."

"Tell him how you feel," I said, simply.

She rolled her eyes and said, "That's easy for you to say, Joseph. You have no idea the horrible things I've said to him over the years. And when he had his stroke..." Gloria choked up. She couldn't finish.

I grabbed her hands and said, "A wise man told me: the only thing that matters is your next decision. I used some choice words with Duke, too. Mom, you need to forgive yourself."

"I guess... I'm just scared. My heart is opening up. And I want to fill it with love again. But, what if too much damage has been done?"

I smiled and said, "Mom, take it from someone who's loved and lost it all. Love isn't time-sensitive. You two had something special. Why not rekindle it while you have a chance? We're lucky to have Duke today. We might not be able to say the same thing tomorrow."

She interrupted, "It's funny you say that. Tomorrow is Duke's birthday."

"I know what I'm going to get him," I said.

"What?" she asked, curiously.

"You, wrapped in a bow," I laughed.

"Oh Joseph..." she giggled.

"We haven't celebrated a birthday in the house for a long time. Let's make it one to remember," I said.

"Duke loved carrot cake. Why don't you pick up the ingredients and some decorations today? We'll surprise him with a birthday break-fast. He'll never expect it," she said, and gave me a wink.

It was 10:30pm before Duke went to sleep. My mother and I were giddy as school kids. I baked the cake, while she blew up the bal-loons and hung the streamers. Our birthday extravaganza was well on its way. I went to sleep around 2:00am and escaped to the sweetest dreams.

The next morning, I awoke to the smell of something burning. I ran up as quickly as I could. I thought the house was on fire. It wasn't a fire. It was my mother trying to cook pancakes.

"You'll have to excuse me, Joseph... I haven't done this in over 20 years. And I was trying to let you sleep in."

"Do you mind if I help? At the rate you're going, we will run out of mix," I joked.

"Do you think he'll like my pancakes?"

"Mom, he's going to love your pancakes."

The concerned look on my mother's face was adorable. She fidgeted around the kitchen, wiping things down, primping her hair, and adjusting her dress. It was like she was going on a first date.

Breakfast was made. The decorations were up and the cake was made. All we needed was the birthday boy.

We heard Duke gingerly making his way down the stairs. I scrambled to pour the orange juice. My mother met Duke halfway up the stairs, and escorted him down. His eyes lit up when he saw the decorations. I pulled Duke's chair out at the head of the table. Gloria helped sit him down.

I grabbed the birthday cake off of the counter and sat it in front of him. We lit all 50-some candles. Duke teared up, as he watched the candles flicker on his carrot cake. We sang happy birthday, in unison. Then, in the sweetest voice, Gloria said, "Make a wish, birthday boy."

Duke closed his eyes for a few moments. When he was ready, we helped him blow out the candles.

My mother served up the pancakes and we sat on either side of my father. We reached out for Duke's hands at the same time, and I led us in prayer.

"Lord, thank you for the half burnt pancakes..."

My mom and dad chuckled at the same time. Then, my mom said, "Joseph O'Dell, be serious."

"OK... OK... God, thank you for family. Thank you for second chances. Thank you for always being there. Thank you for faith. And protect us from the burnt pancakes my mother has so seriously prepared." We all erupted in laughter, and ate breakfast, as a family, for the first time.

We gathered in the living room after breakfast. I sat in a chair and Duke took a place on our sofa. Gloria scuttled off and returned with a gift. She handed the package to Duke and said, "It's for you. I hope you like it."

Duke looked astonished by the sudden show of love and support. He slowly unwrapped the package. It was his favorite book, *Treasure Island*. Gloria said, "I figured I could read a chapter or so a day to you. That's if you want me to, of course."

Duke signaled for her to come closer. He embraced Gloria. She closed her eyes and kissed him on the cheek.

I realized that it was Friday. My father had a doctor's appointment. I retrieved his coat and hat. "Dad, it's time to go to your appointment."

He murmured something that I could barely understand. After repeating it multiple times, I finally got what he was saying.

"Cancel it... staying home... with my wife."

"I'm sure Dr. Weatherby will understand," I said.

Duke whispered something in my mother's ear. She smiled, went to the kitchen, and washed the dishes. Duke signaled for me to come and sit by him. I went to the sofa to figure out what he needed.

"Is everything OK? Do you need a blanket or are you still hungry?"

He signaled for me to come closer. I leaned in and he grabbed me with his paws. He was still so strong. I could feel his tears on my cheeks. Before I knew it, I was crying, too. He pronounced, "Proud of you," in a long, slow drawl.

"I understand. Thank you, Dad. I love you so much."

I sat in my father's arms like a child. It was official. Everything had been restored.

"Joseph!!! Joseph!!! Get up now!!! You have to get up!!!" Bridgett Marie yelled, and shook me violently. I was momentarily unconscious.

Deliriously, I pointed to the ceiling and said, "Hey, gorgeous, you look amazing. I've missed you. I'll be there soon. Can you ask Him for ten more minutes? I should be done by then. She has to hear the story."

Bridgett Marie interrupted, "Who are you talking to, Mr. Joseph?"

I smiled and said, "You wouldn't believe me if I told you. I don't have much time, Bridgett Marie."

Chapter 21

Restored By Faith

A few months passed. It was summer, and Sarah's wedding was only a few days away. We hadn't spoken since that night at the shop. It was sad, and entirely my fault.

Things were looking up everywhere else. I turned O'Dell's back into the creamery my grandfather intended it to be. My parents renewed their vows. And Little PJ visited me every weekend. He finished school and was working an internship.

I was still baffled by the dream I had so many years ago. Everything in my life was restored, but how was Meadow responsible for that? I was so certain, for so long, that we would fall in love, and be the example my family needed.

Maybe it was Meadow's death. Maybe going through something so traumatic gave me the insight I needed to get through to my mother. I reached for different scenarios every day. But none of them fully explained the dream. Most nights, I reconciled myself to the fact that some things weren't meant to be understood.

Standing at the familiar creamery counter one slow afternoon, my thoughts were interrupted by the shrill ring of the phone.

"O'Dell's Creamery, this is Joseph. How can I help you?"

"Joseph, this is Nurse Shauna from St. Mary's hospital."

"How can I help you?" I asked.

In a serious tone, she said, "It's an emergency. I have one of your relatives here..."

Click.

I didn't have time for details. I hung up the phone and rushed to the hospital. All I could think was, 'Why now? Why?' I was supposed to have years of happiness with my dad, not moments. He had suffered multiple strokes and I knew his time was coming. But I didn't want it to be this soon – not when we were finally starting to have a real relationship. I had to get to the hospital in time to say goodbye. I ran through the hospital doors.

"Where's my dad? WHERE'S IS MY DAD?" I screamed.

A nurse finally came to my rescue and asked, "What's your name, son?"

"My name is Joseph O'Dell and I'm here to see Duke O'Dell. I got an emergency call saying he was here."

"Give me one moment, Joseph." She went to the reception desk and spoke with another hospital worker. She walked back towards me with a grim look on her face. "Joseph, please follow me. This woman said you were her only family in town," she said, sadly. I stared back at her confusedly.

"Woman?" I asked.

The nurse led me back to the intensive care unit. I followed her to room number 23. As we approached the door, she touched my arm, and paused before we entered.

"She's pretty weak, and she doesn't have much time," she said.

I walked into the room and discovered Mrs. Kat. She was ghostly white. Sweat dripped from her brow, and her eyes were barely open. Her kidneys had finally failed. The alcohol that she had depended on for so many years was shutting down her vital organs. I grabbed her clammy hands.

"Mrs. Kat, what did you do to yourself?"

"What can I say? I didn't have you around, Joseph," she said, with a weak smile.

"I am so sorry, Mrs. Kat. I should have ignored what you said. I should have tried to take care of you," I said, guiltily.

"I'm stubborn as a mule. And nothing you could have done would have changed my mind. It's my fault. When they told me I was dying, I made them call you."

"I'm so glad you did. I've really missed you," I said, sincerely.

"I missed you, too. And I wanted to say that I'm sorry."

"You don't have to be sorry for anything."

"Yes, I do. Meadow's death wasn't your fault. I thought that you could bring her home to me and make up for some of the terrible mistakes I made."

"I really tried, Mrs. Kat," I said, tenderly.

"It was her choice, Joseph, not yours... not mine. Now, before I go, I have to give you this letter." Mrs. Kat pulled a letter from beneath her blankets and took a deep breath before she continued. "I have been meaning to give you this letter for a long time. I received it a few weeks after Meadow left that last Christmas Eve. I didn't give it to you at first, because I was jealous. She took time to write you, but not her own mother. After her overdose, I read it. But I didn't give it to you then, because I was mad at the world. I'm sorry I held on to it for so long, Joseph. This is for you. Please read it."

My face blanched, and I stumbled to the nearest chair and sat down. Trembling, I opened the letter. It was dated the night I had told her about the dream. The letter read:

Dear JoJo,

I love you, I've always loved you and I knew it early on. I remember when you did your report on me in Mrs. Pittman's class. I never told you, but that was the day you captured my heart. I knew you were good for me. But, for some reason, I always ran to what was bad for me.

You told me, in your shop, that I was not the girl in the backseat. The truth is that I WAS that girl for many years. That is where my father started molesting me, in the backseat of his car. Maybe he did it there so that he wouldn't get caught. Maybe it was a sick fantasy of his... who knows?

All I know is that I don't know how to love in a normal way. I could never believe that someone would want me for anything more than sex. Over the years, I convinced myself that 'that' was all I was good for. Life is tough for me, especially right now. I can't shake the drugs and I know I'm hanging around people who bring out the worst in me, but I don't know how to stop. This can only last for so long. I'm sure that

I'm going to die soon... whether it's someone killing me or me killing myself. Joseph, I just don't want to do life anymore.

I've been with a lot of different men, as you probably already know. What you don't know is that I had a child. I'm not sure who the father is, and, to be quite honest, I don't care. But I'm certain of what I must do for that child now. If something happens to me, I leave you and my mom as guardian of my baby. You were always with me, JoJo. And, when you meet my child, you will finally know how much.

Yours,

Meadow

PS:

You will be amazed at how you inspired my baby's name.

I looked at Mrs. Kat in disbelief.

"Child... What child?" I asked.

Mrs. Kat weakly pointed towards the door, then whispered, "The waiting room... the waiting room."

She sighed one last time, and I knew she was gone.

Reeling from the letter's revelation, hope and trepidation built in my chest. I made my way out of the room and flagged down another nurse.

"Ma'am, do you mind telling me where the waiting room is?"

"It is just down the hall, on the right," she said.

I walked into the sterile waiting room and looked around. To one side, there was a child who looked to be about 5 or 6 years old. The child wore blue jeans and a hooded sweatshirt. The hood was pulled all the way up, obscuring my view. I could clearly see JoJo the bear, held tightly under one arm, and Meadow's red bracelet on the child's wrist. My heart softened even more. I couldn't believe Meadow had kept JoJo, and I thought the bracelet was lost forever.

The kid must have felt me come into the room.

"Are you Joseph?"

"Yes," I said, nervously.

"I've been waiting on you for a long time," the child said, tenderly.

"What's your name?" I asked, curiously.

"My name is Faith."

The child stood up and finally removed the hood. She had blond-ish-brown hair, hazel-green eyes, and an olive complexion. She was the spitting image of her mother. She even had Meadow's dimples.

I fell to my knees as the pieces suddenly came together for me. THIS was the girl of my dreams. The dream was never about Meadow. It was about her unborn daughter, a girl who had no one else in the world. At once, it all made sense... "Have *Faith*... I will wait on you." I had told Meadow this, so many times, with unflagging conviction. But I didn't fully understand what it meant.

In the midst of this epiphany, I recalled the question that Papa Pete had posed so many years ago, "Will you be who you are intended to be?" I thought about Jimmy's words, as Faith and I compared brace-lets. 'Love is indeed the only force strong enough to conquer the grave.' I could finally answer that question Meadow posed to me so long ago. Yes, there is a God. Your daughter is proof. He wanted to build unconditional love and caring in my heart, so that I could be com-mitted to Faith for the rest of my life.

I vowed I would not let her go through what her grandmother or mother went through. That madness would end with my love. I wanted to get out of this town. And write stories that helped people all over the world. But I finally realized my purpose. God had always intended me to be a father to this very special little girl – a girl who would have had no one else.

Faith gazed at me expectantly while my mind raced, and calmly asked, "Are you the man Nana Kat talked about? She promised you would come. Are you my dad?"

Without any pause I answered with all the certainty in my heart.

"Yes, Faith. I'm your dad."

"Daddy, can I have a hug?"

"Of course you can, honey... Of course you can."

<XXX>

"Bridgett Marie, I told you that this was a story about the day I embraced 'Faith'. She was the substance of everything I could have

ever hoped for, evidence of a God I couldn't always see. Chasing after her love would be the toughest thing in the world for me. But, in the end, it was well worth the wait."

Bridgett Marie struggled to pull herself together. The story of a father's love touched her to the core. She finally found the strength to compose herself and talk.

"That is the most beautiful story I've ever heard. But, why are you telling me?"

"This would be a tough day for anyone to fill in, sweetheart. The truth is that I'm dying of cancer and... and..." I broke down. This part wasn't easy for me to get out. I patted my hand on the left side of the bed and said, "Come sit here."

Bridgett Marie laid herself on the bed, next to me.

I continued, "Sarah could never have children, so we raised Faith as our own."

Bridgett Marie interrupted, "But I thought Sarah was going to marry Logan."

"He thought so, too. But that is a story all in itself," I said, with a smile. "Sarah died of MS a couple of years back. I sold off the shop and moved to Tacoma. I wanted her to have the best doctors. The disease claimed her in the end. Faith has grown into an amazing woman. She is married to a great guy, and they have four beautiful kids. I am a proud Papa. She has her Master's in English and is a struggling playwright. She could be anything she wanted, but I always encouraged her to chase her dreams. After Sarah died, she had a job offer to write in New York. But the opportunity hasn't panned out like she thought. And her husband lost his job a couple of months ago. They have really fallen on hard times."

"That is so sad to hear. But I still don't know how I can help."

"I didn't tell her about the cancer until last night. She had enough to worry about. She is on a flight that will be here in a few hours. But my body will quit before she gets here. I can feel it. I never found the right time to tell Faith how she came into my life."

The light dawned in Bridgette Marie's eyes, and she protested, "No... You can't ask me to do it. It wouldn't be right."

"This is more than right... it's perfect. You are my angel. And who better than an angel, to deliver this message? You must tell her the story of how she came to be. Tell her to turn it into a play. That's why it was so important for you to remember the title, 'Have Faith... I Will Wait on You.' The greatest love story no one has ever heard is the story of how my daughter came into my life. Please, Bridgett Marie. Please do this for me," I pleaded.

"I will, Mr. Joseph... I will."

I pointed to the chest and said, "That chest holds the deed to my grandfather's property, my notebooks, poetry, family pictures, my grandfather's art, Pana's napkin, and the letter her mother wrote me before she took her life. Give it to her. Encourage her."

"I will, I promise."

"Now, I have one last thing to write..."

I scrawled feebly across a piece of paper. I announced, "It is finished."

Bridgett Marie folded the note and put it in her pocket. She said, softly, "Mr. Joseph?"

"Yes," I answered, weakly.

"Can I tell you something before you go?"

"Yes, honey."

Tears streamed down Bridgett Marie's face. She placed Joseph's right hand on her pregnant belly. He still had the red bracelet on his wrist. Humbly, she said, "I have a name for my child. JoJo... it works, whether I have a boy or a girl. Is that OK with you?"

With all the strength he had left, Joseph leaned towards Bridgett Marie and kissed her softly on the cheek. He smiled and nodded 'yes', before exhaling for the last time.

Bridgett Marie lay next to him for quite some time. She thanked the heavens for sending Mr. Joseph in her time of need.

A few hours passed and there was a knock at the door.

Knock, knock, knock...

Bridgett Marie answered it. Faith stood there. Her beauty was breathtaking, but tears had carried her mascara down her face.

"Come in, Faith."

"Is my dad here?"

"I'm sorry. He left us just a short while ago. But he asked me to give you this. He wanted you to read it before you did anything else."

Faith took Joseph's final letter and read:

Baby,

I'm already gone. But please don't be sad. I'm dancing with Sarah down streets of gold, in a place where the music never stops. We are looking down on you right now and we couldn't be prouder.

You were my purpose in life and I love you more than anything, Faith. I know you want to come see me. But the real me, my soul, has left. You know that I didn't have much after I paid for your mother's treatment, but I would never leave you empty handed. There is a chest with treasures that will add to a story you must hear.

It is a story that is worth its weight in gold to me. My hope is that it becomes the inspiration for a play, written by you. It will serve as your 'big break', I just know it, honey.

So sit down, relax, and pay full attention to the story Bridgett Marie is going to tell you. I love you with all of my heart. Perhaps, after hearing this story, you will realize even more, how special you have always been.

With all my love,

Your Daddy

Her face full of tears, Faith folded the letter up and placed it back in the envelope.

"My father said, you're going to tell me a story," she said, tenderly.

"Yes," Bridgett Marie said, humbly.

"Does this story have a title?" Faith asked.

"It's called, *Have Faith... I Will Wait on You.*"

"It sounds like a love story," she smiled, tremulously.

Bridgett Marie smiled back; tickled that Faith, herself, didn't catch the double meaning of the title, just yet.

"It is a love story, Faith. It's the greatest love story you never heard..."

Questions to think about

1. Do you believe that everyone is called to wait on someone?
2. Do dreams have an expiration date?
3. Is love an emotion or a choice?
4. Would Joseph have dated Sarah in high school if he hadn't had the dream about Meadow?
5. What does this story tell us about our purpose?
6. If Joseph would have made different decisions, would the outcome of his life be the same?
7. What character do you most identify with and why?

Find out more about the author, view inspirational videos, and shop at jeremyrubinstories.com
Follow us on Twitter @jeremyrstories
Like us on Facebook

Made in the USA
Middletown, DE
19 March 2021

35126435R00117